ENJOY SUCCESSFUL PARENTING

Practical Strategies
for Parents of Children 2-12

by

Dr. Roger W. McIntire

Library of Congress Cataloging in Publication Data
McIntire, Roger W. 1935-
Enjoy Successful Parenting: Practical strategies for parents of
children 2-12 / by Roger W. McIntire
p.cm.
Includes index.
1. Parenting—Psychological aspects.
2. Child-rearing.
3. Parent and child.
I. Title.
HQ755.83.M34   1996   649.1

Published by:

Summit Crossroads Press
11065 Swansfield Road
Columbia, MD 21044-2709
1-800-362-0985
e-mail: SumCross@aol.com
http:\\members.aol.com\sumcross\homepagt.htm

Edited by Sherry Hoffman-Blum, The Right Word

ABOUT THE AUTHOR

Roger McIntire began writing books for parents the day his middle daughter, age six, said, *"My teacher keeps saying we'll run out of time, and we have to stop and clean things up. She says we shouldn't wash the crayons because it wastes time. Daddy, will we really run out of time?"*

Dad said no, but, of course, we will run out of time to raise our children. So Dr.McIntire began writing about the use of family time. From the hours spent counseling families, he compiled lists of examples, dialogues, and principles for using family time so that parents will find the moments productive and enjoyable and yet the growing-up job will be accomplished.

Dr. McIntire has taught child psychology and principles in family counseling and therapy at the University of Maryland for 32 years. He is the author of six books including *Teenagers and Parents, For Love of Children,* and *Child Psychology* (a college text).

In addition to his work with families, Dr. McIntire has been a consultant and teacher of teachers in preschools, grade schools, high schools and colleges. He has published research articles concerning infant vocalizations, eating problems, strategies in elementary school teaching, and high school motivation. He also published several studies of college drop-outs during his tenure as Associate Dean for Undergraduate Studies at the University of Maryland.

Enjoy Successful Parenting presents five guidelines for day-to-day parenting that focus on building confidence and good relationships. Dr. McIntire believes the best chance for a child's happiness is a confident parent who enjoys his\her children and is content with the parenting job.

The Summit Crossroads Press Series
Practical Books Concerning
Child and Family Development

•

ENJOY SUCCESSFUL PARENTING
Practical Strategies for Parents of Children 2-12
•

TEENAGERS AND PARENTS
Ten Steps to a Better Relationship
•

40 TIPS FROM PARENTS
OF YOUNG TEENAGERS**
Messages from Parents Who have Been There
•

SURVIVING COLLEGE**
Practical Guides to Efficient Study Habits,
Strategies for Tests, and Adjustment to College Life
•

Also, a book of humor on the art of working:
CUT OUT MAKE WORK ON YOUR JOB
The How-To Book of Goldbricking

** *To be published in 1997.*

CONTENTS

vi			*Enjoy Successful Parenting*

PREFACE

Parental peace of mind is the highest priority of this book because **the best prospect for a child's happiness is a parent content with the parenting job.** If you can maintain guidelines that lead to a self-confidence that says, *"I handle most situations with my child in a good way, a thoughtful way, and I am in control of my reactions, "* then that contentment will benefit all the family activity.

But useful guidelines for peace of mind will be hard to find, and they run the danger of ignoring complex family situations. Even if guidelines for all child-rearing problems were possible, they would be too complicated to remember, let alone use.

The best compromise I have developed is the list of the five T-rules. These rules can keep parents aware of how their relationship with their children is going while making good progress with communication, teaching, and coaching. And when you feel the need for the support and experience of other parents, the fifth "T" can help you build these and other resources. The Five T's for successful everyday strategies are:

- **TUNE IN** *to What's Going On*
- **TRANSMIT** *the Right Messages*
- **TAKE ON** *Just a Few Good Rules*
- **TEACH** *with Good Listening and Coaching*
- **TEAM UP** *with Adults Who Can Help*

The fifth 'T' may surprise you. But child-rearing in the 90's is more than a one- or two-person job. In the past, families often included relatives who provided help and advice—welcomed or not. Today the extended family is shrinking or gone. That may remove the disadvantage of meddling relatives, but it also decreases their good advice and influence. Modern parents need to know how to control the influence of others on their children, yet get the help and advice they need from other adults. So, a good understanding of the fifth 'T' is crucial.

Each "T-rule" has more than one chapter that will help you keep control, or put you back in control, and help you feel content with the job. At the end of the chapters for each "T-rule," an exercise provides a chance to practice the approach in daily situations. The five exercises can build parent confidence in dealing with daily problems and long-term goals.

The T-rules can also help you remember your good intentions and sort out the possible questions and answers in the present problem. Your good intentions in dealing with your children can get lost in the day-to-day stresses:

> *"I don't want any of this stuff, it's icky!"*
> *"Kathy, those are fresh carrots and they're good for you."*
> *"They look like poo."*
> *"Don't talk like that! Eat your carrots and you can have dessert."*
> *"Poo poo."*
> *"Stop that. Eat your meat if you don't want the carrots."*
> *"All poo poo. Want cereal."*
> *"This is not breakfast, Kathy, and stop making a mess of your food or you'll have to go to bed <u>without</u> supper!"*
> *"Cereal! Daddy doesn't have any carrots."*
> *"Take some carrots, George."*

"No thanks."
"George!"
"What? Making me eat them isn't going to help, maybe we should just get out the cereal."
"Cereal! Cereal! Cereal!"
"Oh, all right, what's the use..."

Mom may wonder if any reaction, short of a parental explosion, would get Kathy to do what's right and leave Mom with sanity *and* a little contentment. For example, for Kathy's bad behavior, should Mom use punishment? What kind? How much? Or should she let Kathy eat what she wants? How far can Mom stand to let that happen? Can Kathy live on just cereal?

And for good behavior (say, Kathy eats a few carrots) Mom should provide encouragement—but how much? Should she bribe Kathy? How about warnings when things are going badly or pointing out there's room for improvement when things go better? In this situation, Mom's threats, warnings (*"you'll go without supper!"*) and bribes (*"you can have dessert"*) produce a peculiar parent-child relationship and cloud Mom's real reasons for trying to get Kathy to eat her carrots.

A good starting point would be a conversation between Mom and Dad about Kathy's choices at supper—without Kathy. Should Kathy choose only from what is served or is a demand for cereal okay? If it is, then having it on the table as a choice would be best. When *both* parents have made a decision, they will find it easier to say, *"This is what we're having for supper."* Kathy may not give up her demands right away, but all the talk about who is eating what will get less attention. Then the family has a better chance of going on to a more enjoyable topic (see "Eating," page 186).

With each reaction, Kathy's mom will encourage, discourage, or have a near-neutral effect on Kathy. Many times children would *like* you to have a neutral effect. At times they will even conspire to convince you that you have *no* effect. The familiar, *"You can't make me!"* or *"I don't care!"* or just plain *"No!"* is their way of struggling to make more room for themselves under the umbrella of limits you are enforcing.

This is a common scheme also used by adults, armies, and nations: tell the opposition they are powerless. Don't believe it. Children sometimes will have their own way and go through their own stages, but remember *your* parents and the influence they had on you, now that you can look back from a distance. Although not always in the direction intended, their effect on your behavior was, and is, real, and your effect on your children is also real.

We don't have time for a thoughtful reaction to every word or action of our children. These everyday behaviors require immediate decisions and judgment calls by the one on the firing line at the moment.

The five T's will help you sort out the pros and cons of possible strategies for dozens of specific practical situations and decide where to focus, when to be strong, and when to relax and allow free growth. I hope this book will help you maintain a sensible and loving balance in your parental reactions, knowing when strong rules are appropriate and when room for more freedom needs to be expanded—again.

Many times this book presents an ideal situation that we all know is only a target to aim for while dealing with the real world. A parent has to take satisfaction in ongoing efforts and be content with imperfect outcomes.

Most of the time, the suggestions and guidelines apply to both genders, and I hope you will understand if I dispense with the cumbersome "she or he" qualifier in most descriptions and use numerous specific examples with each gender.

In this book I have assumed that we want our children to grow up and deal with the consequences of the adult world. **The business is adult-rearing, rather than child-rearing.** We don't want little adults by tomorrow nor do we want our children to miss childhood. But we do want them to mature as the result of experience within the family.

The exercises that follow each of the five parts of this book give you a chance to take an objective look at how your children are dealing with their family experiences. They will also help you maintain an enjoyable family life *for yourself.* In some sessions, you'll be asked to review your priorities and practice some parent skills. As new behaviors come up later in the book, you may want to repeat some exercises, especially the T-1 exercise on what's going on: "The Behavior Chart." The exercises will give you confidence through practice and satisfaction in knowing you are proceeding with a reviewed and thoughtful plan.

T - 1
TUNE IN
To What's Going On

Most parents know a great deal about what's going on with their children, but in the everyday rush, good ideas for helping the situation are often trampled in the hurry and confusion.

The first chapter describes how to observe and understand what's going on and how to plan reactions so that hurry and confusion will not get the upper hand. What's happening? When? What are the usual results?

Chapter Two deals with understanding the blames and credits for what's going on.

1
How to Discover Why
They Act the Way They Do

An employee who tells a joke and gets a laugh will probably tell another as soon as he gets the chance. The teacher who quiets the children by yelling at them, will probably yell more in the future. And the student who gets a break by complaining is likely to be a complaining student again next week. Every employee, teacher, and student is continually making adjustments to the consequences he experiences.

At home, the same rule applies. Although many of your child's habits are made up, in part, by heritage or lingering reactions to events long past, *your reactions*, right now, have the greatest influence. **Of all the reasons for good and bad behavior of children, both genetic and environmental, the immediate results are the most important because parents can adjust their reactions. Other influences are harder to change.**

Take a Close Look at What's Going On

If Brian screams in his mother's ear while she's driving, and the consequence is that Mom scolds him, the scolding has an

effect, but not necessarily the one Mom intended. Brian may have
felt ignored at the moment and he may settle for Mom's attention
in the scolding. If that's the case,
yelling by Brian and scolding by
Mom probably make up a regular
daily routine.

> *Scolding may support,*
> *not reduce, Brian's yelling*
> *and, if so, it's time for a*
> *change—a new strategy*
> *for action.*

If Brian wants his sister to be
quiet, the scolding may have
accomplished that too, even though
no scolding was directed at her.
Again, a regular routine is likely to
develop. Or, the yelling and the scolding may have taken attention
away from his sister. He may repeat the routine just for that. For
any of these reasons, scolding may support, not reduce, Brian's
yelling and, if so, it's time for a change—a new strategy for action.

Perhaps Brian is set up for trouble because he's left with
nothing to do in the car. Bringing along some new toys or games
kept only in the car might help. Maybe Brian needs to know that
scoldings are not bluffs and Mom should say, *"Brian, no yelling in
the car, that's one!"* If Mom gets to three, Mom pulls over and
puts Brian in the back car seat by himself and brings his sister up
front (see "Count-Outs and Time-Outs" in Chapter 9). Maybe
Mom needs to talk more to Brian in the car about things that
interest him—perhaps he needs a little help in practicing
conversation, so he won't be so bored.

Brian:	*"Spiderman!!! Yeaaaaa."*
Mom:	*"Brian, no yelling in the car."*
Brian:	*"Spiderman gets them, Yeah!"*
Mom:	*"Brian, no yelling in the car, that's one. Oh, the trucks are lined up there at the weigh station, more than two!"*

Brian:	*"One, two, three. Three!"*
Mom:	*"Oh! All big ones?"*
Brian:	*"Pretty big."*
Mom:	*"Here's another one, I wonder how heavy he is?"*
Brian:	*"Big."*
Mom:	*"Spiderman could lift him."*
Brian:	*"Oh, yes, and push him out of the way!"*

Does Mom have to keep up the Spiderman level of conversation all the way home? I think so. If Mom were riding with a friend, she would feel obligated to hold up one end of a conversation appropriate for their friendship—it would be a social expectation. Brian deserves the same polite effort. It's harder for Mom to do with Brian, perhaps, but it's not just to keep him quiet. It is his practice of conversation *and* he has Mom's polite effort to imitate when it's *his turn* to start a new topic.

What Are the Consequences of What He Does, The Results of What You Do?

Brian's yelling during driving is dangerous and requires a strategy for action. But most behaviors by the Brians of the world don't deserve any planned consequence. While Brian's volume is a problem, *what* Brian talks about in the car may require only the most liberal limits and strategies. Mom can afford to be tolerant and good-natured and talk about Spiderman if she has sorted the objectionable from the unobjectionable. But if Brian goes in for more yelling, hits his sister, grabs at the wheel, or tries to open the door, Mom needs to take direct action!

Most theories concerning the mysteries of children have a thread of truth to them. All parents have recognized a little heredity in the actions of their children, watched them learn from experience, and have seen the effects of early crucial experiences, both positive and traumatic. **But while all these explanations are genuine parts of child psychology and can help us understand a child, not all explanations are *useful* to parents in everyday situations.** The practical solutions to specific problems *here and now* will have to make use of our reactions *here and now.*

The most useful explanations of behavior deal with a child's encounters with the everyday reactions and consequences from parents and others. Children make daily adjustments to get things to come out better. However, the influences of everyday experiences may be harder to recognize than the constant hereditary and semi-constant "disposition" and "personality" of a child. The motivation for bad behavior can be obscure because it may include a combination of needs not expressed. The child may be hoping for a little solitude, or the opposite—attention, or the

> *To say that nothing can be done is unrealistic because something will be done the next time...*

child might be hoping for a peculiar form of attention such as a sibling's anger. If he annoys his brother, he is entertained by the resulting argument. Another child may need rest, but demand tele-vision time as "rest" provided by a less stressful change of pace.

So the theories and labels can help us understand a child, but may provide little advice about what to do each day. What can you do, for example, when told that your daughter is "hyper-active," "a little slow academically," or "lacking in social skills"? Beyond medication, possibly nothing specific will be suggested except, *"Maybe she should try a little harder."* You might be told "she will grow out of it" or *nothing* can be done because we assume she was born shy, hyperactive, or slow socially.

But to say that nothing can be done is unrealistic because *something will be done* the next time she acts shy, overactive, or makes some social blunder. The parents will react in some way. **Even ignoring the problem is a reaction that has an effect.**

> *Whatever solution Mom tries, the focus needs to be on consequences.*

So in spite of the way they were born or conditioned, children make continual adjustments to the reactions of their parents as best they can, and parents adjust as best they can. One mother turned from a backyard talk with me to deal with her son who was screaming, *"Mommy! Mommy! Mommy!"* Finally she yelled back, *"All right! What is it?!"* He said, *"Hi"* and ran away smiling.

She knew she had rewarded his nonsense with attention he didn't deserve, and she had also given him an additional example of yelling herself, but what was she to do? She turned back to me and shrugged, *"Boys will be boys."*

Yes, he was born a boy and that may have something to do with the yelling, but the explanation shouldn't be used to excuse his behavior nor should it excuse Mom from trying a new way to make things better. Perhaps he should have been ignored—painful as that might have been. Perhaps she should have used the "that's one" approach suggested for Brian's yelling. Whatever solution Mom tries, the focus needs to be on consequences. The choice of consequences and the rules for them come up in *T-3: TAKE ON Just a Few Good Rules.*

Careful Targets with Toddlers:
Why Are the First Two Years Special?

The first two years *are* special. We all know babies are
innocent, and we know their understanding of their world starts at
nearly zero. Parents hope to build communication quickly and
work at it all the time. They also look for signs of successful
communication and marvel at the discoveries of progress.
**Enjoying the successes of a child is *the greatest joy* of parenting
and we usually brag about it:**

> *"Wilma slept through the night almost from the very
> beginning."*
> *"Peter was walking by the time he was one!"*

Our ambitions for our children can make us proud of whatever
they accomplish, but can also lead us into exaggeration because we
want to see progress so badly. And we look for any progress in
understanding so that our job can become a little easier.

> *"It was obvious Terry knew right from wrong even before
> she could talk!"*
> *"She understands 'No!' just fine; she's just ignoring me."*

Exaggerations in the areas of understanding and communication can be dangerous. They can lead parents to rules that are only
confusing to the child and frustrating to the parents.

For the first two years, most behavior needs to be influenced
directly without the use of consequences for learning. For
example, putting dangerous items out of harms' way—not *"letting
her find out for herself"* that pulling on a wobbly chair is
dangerous or that a sharp knife cuts. We can't afford to *"let him*

deal with it" or *"let him follow his own instincts."*

Behavior and personality development in these first years comes mostly from growth and lots of loving stimulation. Learning, of the complex kind, comes later. For newborns, stimulation by holding, cuddling, and talking will do more than provide comfort, it will "exercise" the brain and contribute to development. Needs should be met quickly, "crying it out" makes no sense to a person who barely knows what's the matter, let alone what "being patient" is all about!

For toddlers, parents need to do a lot of "environmental engineering." Remove and put out of sight dangerous and fragile objects. **That will be a lot easier than trying to teach a child the difference between glass and plastic when he has yet to learn the difference between food and dirt!**

Parents of toddlers should be extra careful to separate *the child* from *the action* in both their own minds and in their corrections of the child. Blame is already a sensitive topic! For children under two, even the time-outs of Chapter 9 are not effective. As an alternative, parents could remove the offending child from the situation *and stay with him or her* for a few seconds. The interruption can give both child and parent a fresh start.

What Are the Useful Explanations of Behavior?

For the ages beyond two, explanations of even simple behaviors can be numerous. We need one consistent plan of action that pinpoints the behavior and provides reactions that are appropriate. Careful observation may show that acting "inconsiderate," "tired," or "messy," can be sorted out by the time of day and by asking a few questions.

Parents can ask each other about how the problem developed,

or, in the case of school work, they can ask the *child* questions about school that would tell them if a problem has been frustrating or homework is dreaded.

Armed with more information from listening well (see Chapter 10) both Dad and Mom can react constructively with a rule that says: messy mealtime behavior will result in the messed-up food being taken away for a time, or a rule that says: homework must be done *before* dinner.

Enforcing such rules without exceptions isn't going to create a happy home. But a lack of *any* thoughtful planning is going to leave the child confused at first, and then, with practice, the child will learn to manipulate the outcomes by "acting angry" or "acting tired" when it promises to be to his advantage.

> *The child gains too much control with a "divide and conquer" strategy.*

The worst outcome from lack of focus on behavior and planned reactions is that the parents will disagree and be driven apart. They have their own stake in what happens in each situation and need time together to plan cooperative reactions. **Otherwise, the child gains too much control with a "divide and conquer" strategy or just by taking advantage of the confusion.** With practice, a child can discover strategies to take advantage of unreliable parental habits and the whole interaction can become very dissatisfying and eventually downright destructive to the family.

In the past 30 years, many psychologists have concentrated on changes in individual behaviors. Some believe that because "inside events" such as mental processes and emotions cannot be seen, we should focus on the observable outside events—the behaviors and the reactions to them: what the child does to the world and what the world does to the child in return.

When behaviors are bad, "behaviorists" examine them not as

symptoms of deeper unreachable problems but as the result of
other outside events, the experiences of the child. Obviously there
are disadvantages to a rigid behaviorist's point of view. Children
certainly do have an interior life of feelings, emotions, thoughts,
fears, and joys. Without a consideration of these real events, a
great deal of understanding of children would be lost.

But an approach that is too theoretical is also dangerous
because it tempts us adults to blame it all on what's going on
inside the child (he's rebellious) and we can become overwhelmed
by how complex it all seems (she's at a bad age). **If we conclude
that nothing can be done because of conditions inside, we will
be no help to the child.** We may also miss important events that
happen just before and just after the problem that could be altered
for the better.

Understanding "Why?" by Asking, "What Happens Next?"

As parents, we need to consider what's going on inside our
children to understand their reactions, but we will need to look
outside—among the experiences of the child—to find opportunities to start changes. When Mom asks why her sons Robert and
Billy fight and argue so much, she may expect an answer in terms
of their emotional constitution and other factors such as early
experiences and sibling rivalry.

Of course, these answers are part of the story but if the answer
is to suggest a procedure that would result in a change, the
"Why?" must also be explored by way of another question, *"What
happens next?"*

When parents have a special concern about a child, close
observation will be needed, and the easiest way to do that is to
keep a record of the problem for a week or two. To do this, Mom

used the exercise coming up at the end of Chapter 2. For Robert and Billy's fighting, keeping a precise record on the kitchen bulletin board of the fighting and its immediate consequences was worth the effort because it showed more than just the frequencies of the problem. It showed the likely time of day and trends across days of the week.

To use a chart with these details, you have to single out individual problems. You can only record a few things at once, so select one problem and let the rest go for the time being. For example, Robert's and Billy's Mom marked each time they had a fight. She recorded what attention she gave to the uproar, who deserved the reprimand, time of day, and what the fight was about.

The chart pointed up some aspects of the problem that had gone unnoticed. Fighting happened when things got boring or late in the afternoon when the parents were not available and the boys were hungry. Many fights began just when the parents got home as the boys snatched for attention or became aggravated by the compet-ition for attention while they told their stories of the day. Complicating the situation was the attention that fighting itself attracted.

> *Consequences must be judged by how they influence behavior and not by how we think _we_ would react to the consequence.*

The chart can lead to a new strategy where parents plan to listen and sympathize a great deal just as they get in the door. *"Wait a minute, I have to change and get dinner started"* is not a good strategy here! The chart showed that fighting was used as an entertainment of sorts to fill up the boring moments or that attention from parents, even though negative, encouraged it.

It may seem ridiculous to think that children would fight to be reprimanded by their parents. But one of the cardinal rules about consequences is that **they must be judged by how they influence behavior and not by how** *we* **think** *we* **would react to the consequence.**

What About Billy?
What About Robert?

When the important complaint has been identified, Mom needs to take it apart and focus on the behaviors that make up the problem. These could be unwanted behaviors that are occurring too much or wanted behaviors that are not happening enough.

In Robert and Billy's family, Billy attracted most of the complaints. When not fighting, the complaint about Billy was that he was not neat. However, "neat" is a vague term and is not exactly a behavior; it is a characteristic of many behaviors and not easy to pinpoint when it happens in a six-year-old.

So in this example, before we can go on to look for consequences for neatness, we need behaviors that can be easily identified that define neatness. For Billy, we'll need to specify some of these behaviors so we can zero in and provide a clear message to Billy and so Billy's parents will have a specific activity for their reactions. For instance, they could define "neatness" as: combing his hair, picking up his toys or clothes, and dressing carefully.

Billy's brother, Robert, is complained about for being too aggressive and inconsiderate, and his parents will need a different focus that notes when Robert makes critical and hurtful remarks to others, yells at meals, or hits his brother. Putting the problem in definitions about the observable behaviors of Billy and Robert makes it easier to discover the answer to, *"What happens next?"*

Definitions have three goals:
1. To state the specific nature of the problem,
2. To help specify when consequences would be effective, and
3. To guide the search for the most likely *good* behavior to be looked for first.

This level of behavior must be simple enough and frequent enough to ensure opportunities for support on the *first day* of a new parental rule. And the target behavior must be selected carefully so that Billy and Robert get enough opportunities for reward to see the rule work.

Setting out a "reasonable demand" for performance is tempting, but this may reflect only what the parents think Billy and Robert *should* be doing. We need a positive rule that takes into account what they *are* doing now—reasonable or not. **After things are going well, we can worry about the successive steps necessary to lead them to where they should be.**

> Mom: *"These kids fight too much; it's driving me crazy!"*
>
> Dad: *"And Billy. He leaves stuff <u>everywhere</u>. He's six and it's time he took a little responsibility.*
>
> Mom: *"This bickering has to end. Are they born this way or is it just that something sets them off?"*

Where Mom should place the blame is coming up in Chapter 2. For now, it's best to assume something *does* set them off and try to control the "something" with consequences that follow Billy and Robert's actions:

> Dad: *"From now on, if I have to pick up after Billy, whatever I get goes in the closet for an hour*

> *before he can have it back."*

Mom: *"And whenever they fight, I'm going to separate them for half an hour—TV off!"*

Mom and Dad have begun to control the situation because they're planning with mutual support (more on this in Chapter 15), they are being reasonable about punishments (more on this in Chapters 8 and 9), and they're on their way to sorting out the useful parts of blame and credit (coming up in Chapter 2).

Blame is hard to determine, but what's going on can be figured out without fixing blame. And a reasonable plan for a reaction can change what happens next. In many cases the question of who is at fault may not be useful or even important. **The most useful explanation may be in the question,** *"What happens next?"*

2
Understanding Blames and Credits

We usually give credit for successes, but for mistakes and failure, we distribute the blame in either of two ways: For *our own* mistakes we usually choose "outside blame" that says we are unfortunate victims of situations outside of our control: *"It was so noisy there, how could anyone think or do the right thing?"* "Outside blame" also includes people: *"I was too distracted because people were coming so late!"*

When it comes to the mistakes of *other people (including children)*, we are tempted to use "inside blame." *"What (inside condition) makes him so inconsiderate, so clumsy? Why doesn't she pay more attention? What was she thinking of?!?"*

Where to Place the Blame and Give the Credit

Inside blame is a dangerous habit. Parents should use it carefully. It leads to frustration and inaction because the child is viewed as "having" (inside) a nearly unchangeable character.

Outside blame leads parents to look for problem *situations* instead of problem *children*. **With a good understanding of a**

**problem situation, we have a chance to discover a workable
solution. That, in turn, gives the child a new chance.**

In order to plan reactions to problem situations, you need a
clear view of what's happening. Blaming the child doesn't help
because it's too vague, and it makes assumptions about what is
going on inside. For example, the complaint that Tommy is *"too
demanding and selfish"* refers to real actions of Tommy, but also
says that his demands are intentional and unreasonable. The result
is that the blame has been put inside Tommy, and Tommy's
parents are likely to look for the cure inside Tommy.

Tommy:	*"Daddy! Daddy!"*
Dad:	*"Just a minute, Tommy, I'm listening to your mother."*
Tommy:	*"Daddy!"*
Dad:	*"Just a minute!"*
Tommy:	*"Daddy, I need to go to the <u>bathroom</u>!"*
Dad:	*"What? OK. (Turning to Mom) I'll take him."*
Tommy:	*"I don't need to."*
Dad:	*"You just said ..."*
Tommy:	*"I mean, I don't need any help."*
Dad:	*"Well, just go ahead and go!"*
Tommy:	(From the bathroom) *"Daddy, I need help."*
Dad:	*"I'll be right there."*
Tommy:	*"I'm washing my hands!"*
Dad:	*"So you <u>didn't</u> need help!"* (Walks back to Mom) *"He's so selfish! He wants our attention all the time."*
Mom:	*"Maybe we should forget the selfish part and try to give him attention for other things."*
Tommy:	*"Daddy!"*
Dad:	(Almost losing it) *"What!?!"*

Tommy: *"I went to the bathroom...by myself."*
Dad: (A little tired) *"Good, Tommy."*

Instead of fixing the blame (he's selfish), Mom suggested they look for the reactions Tommy gets for being so demanding. It could be that attention for acting selfish is Tommy's game. Even an argument about his demanding nature could be rewarding. As in Chapter 1, the "Why?" of behavior is again best answered by changing *"Why?"* to *"What happens next?"*

Tommy makes a demand and then what happens? And, when Tommy behaves in non-demanding ways, what happens then? A *useful* answer to Tommy's problem is more likely to be discovered in looking at the outcomes of Tommy's bad behavior *and* the reactions to his good behavior. This focus will lead to a plan to support Tommy's good behaviors and to exercise caution in reacting to unwanted behaviors. Later, when Tommy is having one of his rare moments when he has no demand:

Dad: *"Tell me about this picture you drew."*
(Message: You don't have to act up or make demands to get Dad's attention.)

Useful "blames" (explanations) will not be found in the basic character of Tommy nor in the basic character of Tommy's parents. **The useful answer is most likely found in the common give-and-take between Tommy and his family surroundings.**

Parents should be on the lookout to give credit for the good accomplishments of a child. This seems to be a less frequent family event, because the good behaviors are less well defined, making them less likely to attract parental attention. **Also, the rule of giving credit *only* where credit is due gets in the way of generous support.**

> Elton: *"I got my room cleaned up."*
> Dad: *"Great!"*
> Elton: *"I didn't pick up the parts to my blocks because I'm not finished with the fire station I'm building with them."*

Here's a crucial moment for Dad. His choices are: continue support for what was done; after all, half a loaf is better than none, or, hold out for a higher standard and only give credit when the whole job, with the blocks put away, is done.

> *The rule of giving credit only where credit is due gets in the way of generous support.*

A definition of what is acceptable would help. Doesn't Elton have the option of leaving one ongoing project out? Elton's parents will have to make this judgment regarding Elton's progress and potential, but **the parental habit here should be to err on the side of support—an overdose of support is hard to do in child-rearing.**

Another concern for Dad is what kind of credit should he give. "Outside credit" may be "no credit" (support) at all for Elton: *"I guess the mess finally got to you. Even you couldn't stand it any more."* So Dad shouldn't give the credit to Elton's environment for driving him to do the right thing, and Dad shouldn't take the credit himself by saying, *"Well now, didn't I tell you that would be better?"* Dad should give the credit directly to Elton for getting the job done:

> Dad: *"Well, you still need the blocks out; you would have to just about wreck your firehouse to put it away. You (not me and not other influences) have it looking good in here."*

Looking for Needs and Wants
Instead of Blame and Credit

Recognizing the priorities of needs can sometimes explain the otherwise puzzling fate of some rules. For example, I worked with two very different sisters whose reactions to cleaning up their room was very confusing.

Debbie needed to be constantly assured that her parents thought she was capable and successful, and she tried hard to be cooperative and helpful. Her sister, Susan, also seemed to value her parents' approval but wanted prolonged attention and companionship more than praise.

A rule that reminded their mother to praise both daughters for keeping their room nice worked well for Debbie seeking praise. But since attention ended when the room was done, attention-seeking Susan procrastinated in doing her part just to keep the cleaning going on and on. Susan prolonged the room-cleaning chores for the attention she received—even negative attention would do—while our more goal-directed Debbie worked hard for the confirmation of her success.

Mom may want her daughters to pick up their rooms to keep the place looking nice, but why does she have to be right on top of them while they do it? The reason may be that while she thinks having a nice room is the point of the clean-up (a long-term goal), the daughters' priorities may be quite short-term—one wants assurances that she is contributing (doing it right); the other wants attention for doing any work at all!

Mom has *two* strategies to work on. She carries out one strategy deliberately—encourage them when they clean their rooms; the other strategy is an unintentional one of giving unusual attention to Susan's procrastination. So Susan *slows up* for attention, but Debbie *finishes up* for praise.

The solution for Debbie's and Susan's mother came with the insight that Susan needed attention at the end and long after the chore was completed. This attention did not need to be in the form of praise for room-cleaning; it just needed to continue in order to show Susan that finishing the room doesn't finish Mom's attention.

It would be a mistake to conclude that Debbie wants to please Mom and Susan doesn't. Or that Susan just wants to aggravate her mother. These conjectures about sinister Susan would only lead to more nagging and a sour turn in Mom's relationship with Susan. Mom is the adult, and she had to make the special effort, after room-cleaning, to be interested in Susan.

The Temptation to Blame
in Years Five to Ten

As a child grows up, blaming the person is increasingly tempting for parents. This can distract them from looking for a chance to give good personal credit when it is deserved. For example, you might know an older child who is moody, disrespectful, rebellious, or cynical. Her parents might think of this as a "long-standing habit" (inside blame): *"That's just the way she has always been."* But even older children act the way they do partly because of the way they are treated—because of what has ordinarily happened next.

> *As a child grows up, blaming the person is increasingly tempting for parents.*

Older children may be disrespectful because the only time they are taken seriously is when they act that way. Their bad behavior may produce an entertaining argument, or **their bad talk may seem more "adult" than saying something pleasant. Even some adults believe that!**

When the disrespectful child turns happy and cheerful, adults may pat him on the head and tell him he's a "nice boy" but otherwise ignore him. The usefulness of bad behavior in this situation is not lost on the child.

Showing respect for the child by asking for her opinion, showing confidence in her abilities, and doing a good job of listening (see Chapter 10) will bring out an improved form of respect in return. This strategy, an example to be modeled, encourages social behavior that will replace "disrespectful."

Dad:	*"It's too early to start the garden outside, but we could start seeds inside. What do you think, Elton?"*
Elton:	*"What good would that do?"*
Dad:	*"Later, when we plant them outside, they'll have a head start."*
Elton:	*"Even melons and stuff like that?"*
Dad.	*"Even melons. Let's do melons."*

Where Do the Kids Come Up With These Behaviors !?!

Parents are often amazed at the variety of behaviors—both good and bad—their children show. If you find it difficult to sort out what good behaviors you want, then you can see how difficult it will be *for them* to find out how they should behave. Of all the possibilities, what will they try first in a new situation? Most of the time they will try what worked best for them last time or in a similar situation. **If nothing comes to mind, they may try out what you do! If it works for you, maybe it will work for them.**

Just as you always provide consequences for them, you are also the one they will imitate. Kids may deny it, adults often do, saying we won't do this or that the way our parents did. But then we are surprised to find ourselves acting very much like our parents: *"I can't believe I said that. I sound just like my father!"*

Your parents found the best adjustment for their problems, so you probably went with their choice. Your children will probably follow you, and you will show them the way. When your children agree with you, you will support them. That will be a reward, and another habit, good or bad, will have been passed along to another generation of the family tree!

So it's not always genetics, sometimes it's just plain old imitation. As one mother once said to me, *"I can't understand why my children are fussing at each other all the time. I'm always <u>fussing</u> at them about it!"*

> Mom: *"Carolyn tries hard to be pleasant when anyone in the family comes over to visit. She asked Aunt Mildred if she wanted some of her cookie!"*
>
> Dad: *"I think she takes her cue from you; you always try to make sure everyone is comfortable when company comes. It just rubs off."*

In another case, a father and mother came to me for help in dealing with their son whose main difficulty was his disrespect for others, particularly his mother. "Disrespect" was defined as making sarcastic remarks, ignoring direct questions, and insulting people.

The father said he thought the mother contributed to the problem by being "wishy-washy" and not "standing up to him, even if she is a woman." He thought she probably got this attitude from spending time in "big conferences" with some of her "silly friends." No doubt Dad's disrespect was obvious to his son and provided a terrible model.

It was easy to see where we needed to start. However, the father was surprised that it was with the example he set for his son. The habit had become strong, and the son expected praise and admiration for his behavior from his father. As we will see in Chapter 15, cooperation and support between parents is needed for extra consistency, but it is also needed as an example to children of how to treat their parents!

The Habit of Allowing Practice

Some practice happens by accident; some requires planning. For example, learning to use a spoon at dinner comes from using it in the sandbox as well as at the dinner table. Learning to use words may come from accidental as well as planned practice, or at least planned encouragement *and modeling* from the parents.

Learning to talk comes from conversations and from listening to the reading of stories and comics where imitation is possible. But in reading to a child, practice may or may not be allowed by the parent. For example, asking the child to tell the story of the Sunday comics after the parent has read them would provide practice in talking *and* in imitating Mom and Dad.

Listening itself is not practice. If the comic strip is simple, the child may be able to tell the story without a preliminary reading by the parent. For the more complicated ones, the child can retell them. In this way comics become an entertainment, an enjoyment of talking and telling and learning. **All of this takes more time, but what was the point of allowing time for the comics in the first place?**

When practice has been lacking, painful experiences are ahead for the child. Life has disadvantages awaiting a girl with little

> *When practice has been lacking, painful experiences are ahead for the child.*

experience deciding what to eat, when to eat, what to wear, when to wear it, what to say in making the dental appointment, and when to conserve money. In childhood and teenage years she will feel a little inadequate, dependent, and may question her own worth. As she leaves the family protection, she will need to learn fast in a situation that is not as loving as the family, and she will bring little confidence to the task. **Growing up, that is practicing to be an adult, requires a lot of parent-planned practice.**

As the girl or boy who is "untutored" (that is, unpracticed) leaves for college or work or both, their parents will blurt out a last minute barrage of instructions. Whether practice was left out because it seemed to risk too many mistakes or because it would take too much time in the frantic family activities, parents realize there are consequences to reap and now they rush to get in all those cautions: *"Make sure you brush your teeth, comb your hair, get your rest, start your checking account, and choose friends wisely!"*

> *The only place there is love enough for all that practice is in the family.*

The first experience of being away from home can be all the more difficult and lonely if our offspring-now-sprung has little confidence in deciding what to wear, when to study, and when to rest. Many of my college students go to a campus counselor with the complaint that no one seems to care about them at the big university. A great deal of the "care" the student misses should have been withdrawn years ago to make room for practice and pride in self. **The only place there is love enough for all that practice is in the family.**

One of my students complained about doing his own laundry because he didn't understand all those selections of cycles and what to wash with what. He was embarrassed to say all his underwear was now pink! I joked that he could throw away his socks and underwear when they got dirty and buy new ones. Taking me seriously, he cried, *"I don't know my size!"* For 19 years the washing instructions and the little number on the back elastic of his underwear followed him around, but he had no need of it as long as Mom did all his laundry *and* shopping.

Most of my students managed to survive the passage from home to campus despite painful evenings learning their size and how to use a washing machine. So lack of practice didn't cause a great deal of permanent damage.

But in many cases, a critical period of childhood that would have nurtured a knowledge of self-worth and a comfort with life was missed. Later, *complete* development of self-contentment may be difficult or impossible to secure.

Exercise and Summary for T - 1
TUNE IN On What's Going On

The Behavior Chart

The five exercises in this book are designed to help you clarify and organize your own view of child-rearing. In the later exercises, I hope you will customize the ideas in these chapters to your own philosophy and your daily parenting.

Behavior Charts will be a good future reference and a good record for sorting out what's going on in each situation. Blank Behavior Charts are provided at the end of this exercise.

Fill In the Seven Steps of a "Behavior Chart"

The first exercise creates "behavior charts" so that the questions of *"What happens next?"* and where to place the blames and credits will be clear in your mind when the troublesome situation comes up. You may need to return to this exercise to make new behavior charts as you focus on new situations. For this first session, examples are provided for each part.

Step 1: Describe the problem objectively.

Often this provides more help for the parent than other parts of the exercise. Just putting down what exactly is bothersome allows Mom and Dad to pick their attention targets and find room for positive support when it is deserved.

Example: Fred always disrupts dinner, makes noises, cries, complains about the food, and wants down off his chair.

Step 2: What triggers the action?

Think back to the last few times the problem in Step 1 hap-pened. What started it all? Who was involved? What time of day was it? Does it always occur in a certain part of the daily routine—bedtime, meals or when siblings are absent?

Example: Happens when dinner is late and I give him something to "hold him over." Or, "Didn't happen when his sister was at grandma's."

Step 3: What happens next?

You may have to think back to some of the last moments of the problem to remember exactly what ordinarily happens right after the troublesome behavior. Long-term consequences can play a role, but we need to understand the immediate effects first.

Example: We usually try to get him to eat, tell him to stop acting up, sometimes let him down since he just dawdles along and makes trouble anyway.

Step 4: Where would you place the possible blames and/or credits?

Sometimes this part will not apply to the subject at hand. But often an objective statement about where each person thinks the fault lies will direct us to action without having to badger the transgressor with blame.

Example: He's just trying to get attention and he eats junk between meals. It may also be a power game.

Step 5: At what age would you expect an average child to do what you are hoping will be done in this situation?

Don't skip this part. Often when parents consider the age

they would expect an ability to develop, they realize they
are ahead of the child's schedule in their demands and
expectations.

**Example: He's four. He should be able to eat at the
table without making extra trouble.**

Step 6: How could we allow more practice?

Is it possible to provide more opportunities for the child
to try out appropriate behavior with your loving support
handy?

**Example: He needs more practice in conversation
with appropriate topics when he is at the table. We
also should stop the junk food between meals.**

**Step 7: When do problems occur? Keep a record similar to
the one on the next page.**

A short record of what's going on and the effect of your
reactions is often a good starting place for pinpointing a
problem. Use or copy the blank behavior chart at the end
of this exercise and try to keep a record for a week so
that you can review a good sample of the action.

A Sample Behavior Chart

Date/Time	What happened?	Just <u>before</u> this?	What happened next?	Special situation and remarks
Mon/ breakfast	Cried/started hitting	Ran out of his juice	Told him to try other juice	Bad night's sleep
Mon/lunch	Went OK, he talked about preschool	Had preschool	He watched TV while I cleaned up	
Mon/dinner	Went OK, once he had the toy he wanted at dinner	Playing by himself	We watched Sesame Street together	Sister was away at friends for dinner
Tues/all meals	Not good/ fighting, not eating	Morning shopping	Put him to nap after lunch, he cried	Shopping always makes him tired
Wed/all meals	Good/no problems	Good weather, he played outside	Went back outside	Things always go OK when he gets outside

Date/Time	What happened?	Just before this?	What happened next?	Special situation & remarks

Date/Time	What happened?	Just <u>before</u> this?	What happened next?	Special situation & remarks

T - 2
TRANSMIT
the Right Messages Every Day

Friends and Searchlights

Friends bring out the best in me. When we meet, their attention sweeps the common ground between us looking for sparkles to highlight. I like the "me" they draw out. I return the compliment, like a friendly searchlight, seeking the best in them.

Some people have another focus. Their search overlooks the good I try to provide and zeros in on vulnerable spots. I pull back and risk very little because I know what they're looking for. I cover up.

Parents and their children should be friends. Not in the sense of enjoying the same music or having friends in common or playing similar roles in the family, but in the sense of enjoying time together and looking for and supporting the strengths and successes in each other.

Aim *your* searchlight carefully.
What are *you* looking for?

3
Daily Messages That Catch 'em Being Good!

The good in some people is hard to find, and our inclination to criticize them can easily outweigh any temptation to praise.

In families, it's not always that good behavior is absent, but that a parent's lack of clear definitions for good behavior provides no cues as to when to react with praise. We parents know very well what bad behavior is: fussing, fighting, making messes, and doing dangerous things. But the words we use for good behavior are often less specific: "be nice" and "act right." **Not having an exact idea of what good behavior should be, we have trouble finding it.**

The search is all the more difficult if "good" is described by what we *don't* want: *"Don't make trouble, don't yell at your sister, don't act like a trapped monkey in the back of the car."*

Descriptions with "not" and "don't" in them are hard to use. *When* should you react to "*not* fighting" or "*not* fussing?" And when these bad habits are finally abandoned, what is a child _to do_? What should a parent look *for* in a child's choices of action?

Better to think of specifics—help with setting the table, saying something complimentary to your sister, giving your brother a toy he's been looking for.

Vague expectations about good behavior and specific descriptions of bad, can lead to the common situation of unbalanced parental reactions with bad behavior attracting most of the attention.

Being specific about good behavior leads to new advantages:

1. **Parents become alert and react to** the small successes that are part of larger ones.
2. **Children get clear messages** about behavior.
3. **Parents provide good examples** of how to encourage others.
4. **Children develop and improve** with small easy steps instead of becoming discouraged by reprimands for small mistakes.

Pinpointing the Small Successes

A "catch 'em being good" rule puts parents on the lookout for their children's successes and the good behaviors that will allow them to give more support. These successes are usually just small parts of the larger habits of their children. For example, considering how to encourage a child who is "shy," is a complex problem because such an over-used and abstract concept of a person does not explain the little events from the average day that make up the impression of "shyness." It is too large and covers too many emotions and habits.

We need to know what behaviors to look for in order to pinpoint what is worrisome and when to react. **Without the pinpointing, the temptation is to try to *talk* the child out of being "shy."** *"Oh, come on. There's nothing to be afraid of* here!" "Just say hello." "Go over with the others. What's your problem?!"

If the problem is restated in specific terms: *"He doesn't talk very much"* or *"She hides when company comes"* or *"He likes to play alone,"* then the appropriate reaction to each of these habits can be worked out. That way, parents will know when they want to encourage change (*"we'll encourage her a lot when she has something to say"*) and when to avoid the risk of embarrassing, unwanted attention (playing alone is OK). Also,

> *Avoid sending the message that she should be ashamed of her own personality.*

focusing on a few good behaviors replaces the habit of blaming the whole child, "putting her down," and sending the message that she should be ashamed of her own personality.

Too often complaints deal with behaviors we want to reduce or eliminate. Complaints about absent behaviors that are desirable are not as common as complaints about unwanted behaviors that are easier to see. It's easy to complain about a shy child who cries when strangers come, but what reactions can be expected if the child does "come out of her shell?" Shyness produces some attention with little reprimands and excuses. What does non-shyness produce?

A careful parent might plan some mild encouragements, and even practice what could be said in a planning session, *"That was a nice 'Hello.'"* With a plan to provide attention for those non-shy moments, things might improve for the patient parent. The child's request to get away from the visitor might be answered with, *"OK,"* avoiding additional begging by the parent to get her to stay or begging by the child to get away.

Learning to Practice and Practicing to Learn

The focus on good behavior identifies the specific practice that is likely to lead to improvement.

Children (and adults) learn by doing—by practice. Practice allows trial and error in the protection of the family where parental encouragements can consistently motivate more practice and emphasize the benefits of better behavior. If parents work out more exactly what is happening and what they want to happen, then they can apply this fundamental law of learning: *"One learns what one does!"*

> *The main role of a family is to provide a place where successful practice will be supported and mistakes will receive only constructive reactions.*

Anyone who has ever tried to play a musical instrument, improve in a sport, or raise children knows that just talking about it is not enough. Readings, lectures, and memorizing rules can help, but real practice is crucial! It's true that even golf has helpful hints and rules to learn, but all golfers know the only way to improve is through practice. And all golfers know players who still search for the magic gadget or secret technique for success while they avoid practice time. **The notion applies equally well to social behavior, controlling anger, getting along with siblings, homework, tooth-brushing, and money management!**

So helping a child listen and pay attention to advice is not enough, he will have to try out your instruction, test your rules, and then, if the consequences and encouragements are there, he will learn. The progress itself—the result—will have to come from practice.

That is the main role of a family—to provide a place where successful practice will be supported and mistakes will receive

**only constructive reactions—not a likely experience in the
outside world.** The family should provide an opportunity for safe
practice without cruel punishment for mistakes and with a person
who cares enough to support small successes. Supportive family
members will be hard to come by when the child grows up.

Practice Makes Almost Perfect

Many parents realize the importance of practice and tell their
children to "work hard" in school. The details of school learning
will be taken up in Chapter 13, but the important notion of practice
has a role in all parts of learning. The "work hard" idea is good
advice but, by itself, leaves out the specifics. Children need to be
shown the particulars of the practice.

**Successful work shows up in grades if the student is shown
how the "work hard" idea is turned into active practice—not
just staring at pages, but reading aloud; not just "trying to
remember," but talking to others about the work, drilling
important concepts, rewriting notes and important material,
and drawing new diagrams or tables that organize facts
differently.** That's how the idea of "work hard" becomes
successful learning.

If you are skeptical of this strategy, try the following
experiment:

> Pick out a favorite magazine in which there are two articles
> or stories you have not yet read. Read the first story to
> yourself in your usual way. Find someone to listen to your
> report of the story or article and tell them all the detail you
> can remember—who wrote it, who was in it, what was
> going on, conclusions reached, and so on.

Now go back to the magazine and read the second article or
story. This time, stand up, and read out loud, with good
emphasis and inflection—to the wall, if necessary. Now
find your listener again and report this story, giving all the
details you can remember of who, what, and where.

By the end of the second report, you will notice how
much more you remember of the second story. As one
student said to me, *"Well, of course I remember that one,
I remember what I said!"*

For learning and changing habits, there is no substitute for
active practice. **On your vacation, stare at pages in a novel
while lying on the beach if you enjoy it, but if it's for learning,
"work hard through practice."**
We'll be back to the most important application of the practice
notion when the strategies for success in school come up in

Chapter 13. And we all understand the necessity for practice when teaching something new.
But when we are not thinking of schoolwork,
tying shoelaces, playing the piano, or hitting a
baseball, we often forget this essential
ingredient. It applies just as well to bed-
making, dish-washing, and manners in society.

**We shouldn't
wait until
she's ready
to do it
without a
flaw—that
day may
never come.**

If you do these jobs for your children, there
is no practice. It is easy to be overprotective
and slow down learning: *"I'll cut the meat,"*
"I'll pour the milk," "I'll read, you listen," and *"I'll call and see if
your friend can come over—you wait."*

Some parents will protest that if they let their child do these
things, mistakes will happen. She might cut herself while cutting
the meat, spill the milk, waste time reading instructions, or say the
wrong thing on the phone. All true. And each parent will have to

make the judgment—is she/he ready? Not, *"Is she ready to be perfect?"* But, *"Is she ready to gain <u>something</u> from practice and mistakes?"* We shouldn't wait until she's ready to do it *without a flaw.* Without practice, that time may never come.

> *A wise parent creates practice, not just for learning, but to improve the child's self-respect.*

Another advantage to early practice is that your child can gain much to be proud of *now.* It's true we can't give a steak knife to a two-year-old or a gallon of milk and a small glass to a four-year-old, but we need to set up practice situations so that we can guarantee opportunities for encouragement and praise. A wise parent creates practice, not just for learning, but to improve the child's self-respect. A butter knife for the bread, a small pitcher for milk, a chance to "read" (tell about) the picture in a story, and call a friend just for fun—all of these are steps that promote learning and increase self-esteem.

Use Small Steps and Big Rewards

When you were growing up, practice seemed to be enough to perfect your handwriting. And yet in learning to play a musical instrument, you may have found that even practice was not enough. **What are the differences between your brief piano experience and your "learned forever" handwriting?**

In learning to improve your handwriting, you were rewarded not only for the hours of practice but also for the first little successes. You wrote your own name, a friend's name, then a secret message, a note to a friend, then a letter to Grandpa. The improvements were useful, shared with others, and practice continued.

But too often the first improvements in playing the scale on the piano produce little or no admiration, they seem of little use, and are a long way from the performance dreamed of. Sometimes piano lessons are successful because learning a favorite piece or popular song was part of the early training. If that consideration was a part of your lessons, practice probably continued. If not, you may have quit, but **I bet you remember to this day the pieces you liked, that attracted some attention, and that others enjoyed.**

If rewards come early for the first little successes, then a child will want to practice more on other small steps. If only big successes attract encouragement and little improvements are ignored, a child can become discouraged along the way: *"I'll never be really good."* **It is not the pot at the end of the rainbow that keeps the practice going, it's the next pat on the back or penny in the bank**—and for some tasks, parents need to be the frequent and generous back-patter.

> *Some kids need more physical love, like hugging, than others. Most parents err to the side of too little.*

The generous back-patter should also find the right amount of shoulder-patting, touching, and all-around hugging. Some kids need more physical love, like hugging, than others. The inclination of most parents is to err to the side of too little.

Aim a little higher. Remember, they're born with an instinct to act independent. Before you are discouraged by a child who pulls back a little from physical contact, look at the effect over the weeks. This part of your relationship will always need adjustment, and the need for more is the most likely.

The most common error when beginning to teach something new is to demand too much for too little. The first steps need big rewards—not necessarily tangible goodies but plenty of encouragement. *"This sounds like bribery,"* you might say. *"Shouldn't a child do most of these things without contrived rewards—can't they do it just for the love of learning?"* *"Some children are good and do what is expected without 'rewards,' don't they?"*

To answer these questions we need to realize that those good little children *were* rewarded—socially and with parental respect and praise—a great deal. Some children start early and do well, with plenty of encouragement. They perform so well that they receive a great deal of praise and a snowballing effect begins that is an advantage for years to come. **If a child starts off with good encouragement and is well rewarded, he keeps going. If she keeps going, she is further rewarded and so on.**

Snowballing can work the other way also. Some children don't receive rewards or attention for the first steps to good performance and learning. They don't expect rewards because few were given in the past. They might do just the minimum out of fear, but they will remain at the minimum and even that will disappear when the threat is gone.

So without someone providing positive feedback, the child misses out on encouragement. As the child falls further and further behind his parents' expectations, any performance that should have been encouraged earlier will be ignored because *"He should have done that long ago."* Now even meager attempts at catching up are discouraged. If his success is viewed as "too late," the "pay" may be nothing. Without some "pay" he will fall back even further.

Stanley: *"These math problems are really hard."*
Mom: *"You're really getting into some hard stuff now."*
             (see "Reflective Statements" in Chapter 10)
Stanley: *"Yeah, they take too long."*

Mom: *"You got the first one. You should show your brother."*

Stanley: *"Hey, Larry, look at this!"*

Larry: *"We did those last year."*

Mom: *"And they were hard, but Stanley got the first one."*

Stanley: *"I'll try one more."*

Mom's intention here is just to show respect for what Stanley has done so far, and a little encouragement to show it off. Larry doesn't help much, but Mom remains on the positive side and Stanley puts in a little more effort.

Does this mean that all successful parents are secret bribers? No. First, these words are unfair because they imply a situation in which a person is trying to corrupt another person to do something wrong and usually illegal. Second, a child is not expecting a "bribe" just because she expects some return for her effort. No one works for nothing. Some volunteers work for no money, but they receive a satisfaction that is rooted in the reactions of others. The reward may be as subtle as another person's compliment or as obvious as salaries for Congress and fees for doctors and lawyers.

In addition to practice, kids need recognition, respect, and encouragement.

In the adult world of raises, benefits, and strikes, the importance of the consequences for our efforts is always there. On one occasion a father rejected my suggestion for encouraging his son's homework by saying. *"He should be grown up enough to want to do the right thing without some payoff!"*

When it came out that the father was on strike for more money *and* was getting support from a strike fund, his defense was that *he was an adult*! With his experience and knowledge he felt he deserved a tangible reward (as well as admiration and respect). **His son, without experience, without success, and without respect, was to take his responsibilities for the love of it.**

So in addition to practice, kids need recognition, respect, and encouragement. With all the right ingredients, the success will come *and*, along with it, a bonus, self-respect.

Short-Term Benefits and Long-Term Goals

Adults are taller; they can see farther ahead. While sorting out what happens next, both immediate and delayed reactions need to be considered.

Mom: *"Why does she go running out of the house without a jacket? She knows she gets a cold every time!"* (Ah yes, but that's *later!*)

Dad: *"My friend, George, is just like that at work. He snacks all the time, he's overweight, and he can barely climb a few stairs without panting. Someday he'll be a death-due-to-donuts! Can't he see what he's doing to himself in the long run?"* (That's later, also, and George gives in to the "right now.")

Teacher: *"I run two miles every morning. Sometimes it's hard to get started on it, but I feel better afterwards."* (Somehow this teacher resists the effects of inconvenience right now for a better feeling later. How does she do that?)

Brian: *"It's a good TV night, but if I attend every Scout meeting, I'll get points toward a merit patch!"* (Here's a hint about how long-term benefits come to work: there's a *short-term* benefit!)

Behaviors tend to follow the short-term benefits at the expense of long-term goals, but with a few positive experiences, long-term consequences can overpower temporary temptations, especially if someone supports the effort. How can a parent help this process of considering the long-term benefits of good behaviors and the long-term problems of bad ones?

A common parental strategy is to try to talk a child into considering the long-term. Talk by itself is often not enough as most of us dieters know. We need some symbol of the long-range goal *right now*, a reminder that we are making some progress—a daily chart with marks for successes, a record book, or diary. Children may need something more concrete such as stickers, buttons, Scout badges or treats.

> *We all know how our morale is elevated by bosses who are positive and supporting and deflated by ones who only react to mistakes.*

If those little encouragements are given, they can have an effect on the present behavior. Isn't that what compliments from the boss, new titles or privileges at work, promotions, and badges in the military are all about?

Many positive reactions in the here and now are not contrived tokens, badges, or promotions. They are simply people on the lookout for opportunities to compliment and praise the small steps of good habits. It's not an easy task to be so observing and responsive, but those that do it have a good effect. We all know how our morale is elevated by bosses who are positive and supporting and deflated by ones who only react to mistakes. **When work and chores are only for long-term benefits, a "boss" needs to put in short-term encouragements that keep up the good effort!**

Making Plans for Non-Behaviors

Be careful when planning consequences for *non*-behaviors. Rules that say, *"If you don't do such and such* (watch too much TV, act too shy, walk on the flowers, hit your sister) *I'll reward you"* are difficult. The time of the promised reaction may be too arbitrary. When does *not* watching too much TV happen? Better to build your rule around the *alternative* to TV—something that happens at a particular time and gives you an opportunity to support your son or daughter at a particular moment: *"You're working on your picture, it's looking really good!"*

Non-behavior rules not only fail the specific time test, they also fail to tell the child exactly what *to do*. The solution to the non-behavior complaint can be reached by searching for what the child *should* be doing. *"Karen watches too much TV"* needs to explore what Karen *should* do. Karen's parents would be at a loss to keep her busy every moment but it's a situation where the *extent* of TV is the problem. Karen's parents could plan some encouragement for a few alternatives to the tube.

Does this mean that Karen's parents should load up on toys, candy, and money to lure Karen away from TV? Probably not. Most parents have found these rewards to have temporary effects —except in the case of money which will become a bigger part of Karen's life soon enough without any help from us.

> *Non-behavior rules not only fail the specific time test, they also fail to tell the child exactly what to do.*

For problems such as Karen's, we need to look around for something useful that we might encourage her to do that would have the advantage of making Karen feel a little more important. She might even be proud of doing some of the drudgery of life. How about dusting, setting the table, cooking, sweeping, cleaning, or painting. Painting? *"But she won't do it right!"* you might say. *"She'll mess it up. Cooking? That must be a joke."*

Of course it's true that you could do any of these tasks better than your child. To get it done right, do it yourself. But the purpose here is not just the job itself, it's the self-esteem, the learning, and the alternative to TV. **How well the job is done is not a priority.** Now don't forget to plan the consequences: your time, positive attention, and some hugs and back-patting.

4

Daily Messages that Create
the Family Atmosphere

Everyone contributes to the family atmosphere. Each
contributor also follows the lead of the others—modeling,
imitating, and reacting in a manner appropriate to past experience.
Respectful, loving parental reactions are copied by the children in
their responses back to the parents and on to others. The social
habits of the children and the parents recycle through the family,
creating the general atmosphere as these habits are repeated.

Sending the Right Messages

Before we move on to the general philosophy of how to make
rules in Chapters 6 to 9, let's examine what general philosophies
are already at work in shaping the family atmosphere.

How easily and how frequently do you react to your children?

Everyone has seen parents who are always riding their
children: *"Blow your nose." "Tuck in your shirt," "Don't touch,"*
and so on. On the other hand, we have all seen parents who *never*

react and let their children run wild with no consideration for others or their property. Both extremes lead to problems. Where, in the middle ground, is the right level of correction? The answer here is in the *nature* of all of these little corrections.

Parents who use frequent, *but positive*, reactions to their children usually have a positive, and less frantic, family situation. **A mother who tends to support, encourage, agree with, and reward or compliment frequently is much more influential and closer to her children than Mom, the critic.** Yet criticisms are necessary because every child continually explores limits and if there are none, behavior quickly gets out of hand.

Messages About Loving a Person, About Liking a Behavior

The frequency of criticism sends a message about how parents feel about their children. Do they love them? Of course they do! But how can their children tell if their parents *like* them? You can get an impression of the *liking* by the frequency of those little criticisms. Liking is expressed by the accumulated parental reactions to what the children do, and they are always doing something! So the message about liking is updated very frequently in reactions to everyday behaviors.

Loving is not expressed as often and messages about how you love your children are greatly outnumbered by messages about how you like them. It's important to be sure that the frequent reactions are sending the right messages.

Mom: *"Leave Baby Mark alone, Charles."*
Charles: *"I was just going to pat him."*

Mom: *"I know what you were going to do. Now just stay away, you will wake him!"*

Mom: *"I like to pat him, too. But it will just wake him up and he's tired."*

Charles drops his jelly sandwich:

Mom: *"You are so messy! Look what you did!"*

Mom: *"Oh, look what happened! Better pick it up and get a towel."*

If Mom chooses the comments on the left, she emphasizes Charles, the person. *You* will wake him, *you* are messy. If she chooses the comments to the right, she emphasizes a third thing that she and Charles are dealing with, which is Charles' behavior and its results: *It* will wake him. Look *what* happened. **It won't make a lot of difference to Charles on this one occasion. But over the long haul, Charles ends up with a very different message and a very different relationship with Mom.**

The emphasis on the defects in the person acts as a punishment. Jovial and approachable people never seem to punish. They have a rule that says, *"When mistakes happen, emphasize outside events"* (see "Use *It* instead of *You*" in Chapter 10). To the extent that they must correct, contradict, reprimand, and punish, they risk losing this friendly air. **This can be one reason some growing daughters and sons become alienated from family and would rather go outside with friends or stay in their own rooms. It's the likelihood of**

> *Over the long haul, Charles ends up with a very different message and a very different relationship with Mom.*

**criticism, "put downs," and corrections that drives them
away—just as it does Mom and Dad:**

Mom: *"John, sometimes I wonder if you really like me,
        you criticize me so much!"*
Dad: *"Honey, I love you!" You know that."*
Mom: *"That's different. That's not what I hear during
        the day."*
Dad: *"What? You want gush and mushy stuff all the
        time?"*
Mom: *"No, I just want the benefit of the doubt. I want
        someone on the lookout for my good points and
        my successes. I've already got plenty of critics in
        my world!"*
Dad: *"You have plenty of good points."*
Mom: *"Then point them out now and then."*

Praise, encouragement, and genuine friendliness are no doubt
the most effective influence spouses have. And the same good
influences work on their children, too.

> *Selecting behaviors
> to reward with
> positive attention
> is the main business
> of being a parent.*

When these reactions are used consistently in a direct way we get results. Your
child attracts your attention easily—for
good or bad behavior. Therefore, when
paying attention to a child, deciding what
should attract your attention and what
should not is important.

**Selecting behaviors to reward with positive attention is the
main business of being a parent.** Use your good sense and the
exercises in this book (especially those at the end of Chapter 5) to
keep your attention on target. Your habit will be contagious and
the whole family atmosphere will be more positive.

If looking for mistakes becomes the routine, parents become unpleasant when doing the parenting job and don't like themselves as they do it. The children will respond in kind and avoid the family when possible. **It cannot be emphasized enough how much your positive attention influences your children and others.**

Children engage in a conspiracy—almost unconsciously— to show you that you are having no effect. They don't have the insight or assertiveness to have conversations like the one above between Mom and Dad. But don't be misled. It may not show up in the short run, but your reactions do make *the* difference. Don't give up. Watch a certain behavior for a few weeks to test your influence and notice how upset they get when they feel ignored! Attention, praise, and general encouragement are handy rewards. They can be used often.

> *Children engage in a conspiracy—almost unconsciously—to show you that you are having no effect.*

Another Side Effect of Frequent Criticism

In reacting to everyday problems, children most commonly imitate the adults they are with at home and school, and they imitate style more often than the specific adult behaviors. Attitudes toward others, conversational style, and temperament are the durable characteristics of teachers and parents that are copied. The result is a general disposition made up of habits and styles of encouragement or punishment of others. **A child can easily acquire a disposition almost entirely from the family air!**

The disposition to punish and correct others can be learned just as easily as the disposition to encourage others but the results are vastly different. Punishment shows that out of all the responses the child could have made, he has chosen the wrong one—try again. Little information is available in that.

A positive reaction is much more efficient because it says that of all the things he could have done, this is one of the right ones. A rewarding reaction is more difficult for parents to come up with, however, because they must take time to decide what they want to reward and what comment or material thing to use as reward. We're more likely to already know what we want to punish and how we would do it.

The positive approach emphasizes reward—not necessarily material ones, but approval, smiling, etc. You have a more pleasant job as a parent and you have a child who is still informative, friendly, responsive, and not always wanting to go somewhere else! The choice between rewards and punishments will be taken up in detail in Chapter 8 and 9, but in most cases the odds favor reward.

Learning to police your disposition is a difficult task. No one is planning consequences for *you* as an adult, and adults change by practice with encouragements just as children do. So whether or not anything can be done about the dispositions in your home depends on the answer to the question: *"Can you control yourself through conscientious effort and through feedback from your partner?"*

If you are a single parent, it may be all the more difficult to say to yourself, as a spouse might: *"Don't let me pick on the kids; stop me and point out my good reactions."* Chapter 15 takes up the strategies of going it alone.

The disposition of the children and the whole family can also be influenced by planning for the small everyday social behaviors of kids. Many parents have developed a poor disposition in their child by not expanding the limits of *their own expectations* as carefully as they plan the limits on the kids. For example, in what situations will the child be on his own? A child makes so many mistakes, there are so many things we want him to do right, and so many things he can do wrong.

Without planning, parents feel that they have to be after the kids constantly and one parent may complain to the other, *"Why can't you just leave him (her) alone?"* The answer is that, without a plan, Mom or Dad cannot be sure what "right" should be encouraged and what "wrong" should be discouraged. They can't leave the child alone because they *always* find the problems.

Amazing Copies!

"Isn't it amazing how mother and daughter are alike!" said Ms. Jones. *"That woman reading at the end of the back row just has to be Regina's mother. Regina even reads at lunch time!"*

"Yes, it's unbelievable," whispered Ms. Miller. *"I would recognize Bobby Comic's father anywhere with his attempt at a little joke. And Lisa Sour's father sulking while he waits for the meeting. You wouldn't believe such details could be inherited!"*

Ms. Jones and Ms. Miller were teachers at PTA back-to-school night. They told me that when they were waiting for the meeting to start, they played a "Match the Parents Game." It's been their favorite for years, and they find their guesses to be very accurate. Their success with matching parents and students comes, in part, from physical similarities that are inherited, but the way the students act is partly a copy of their parents' style. It's a hint the teachers find very useful in their game. How talkative, pleasant, sarcastic, or happy each parent and student is, helps the teachers make their matches, and they are very successful!

A Disposition Creates
Its Own Surroundings

When children imitate bad dispositions, they must use threats in a subtle way because they are less powerful than adults. Fighting back, a child puts off her parents or teacher and reduces their requests for work. She creates further reactions that are viewed as confirmation of her cynical expectations of others.

Consider Lisa, eight years old. She has developed a negative attitude. Most of the time at school she is cynical and pessimistic. You can imagine that it is easy to feel uncomfortable or aggravated around her. At home with her family, Lisa receives a bit more attention, but the aggravation and frustration that others feel usually shows through:

> Mom: *"How was school today, Lisa?"*
> Lisa: *"OK"*
> Mom: *"Well, tell me about it!"*
> Lisa: *"Do you have to know everything?"*
> Mom: *"I was just interested."*
> Lisa: *"Just leave me alone."*

Lisa is a non-rewarder, thinking little of others and asking little from them. She's no trouble, but somehow she's still troublesome. **She brings out the worst in others and then reacts to that by getting worse herself. The cycle continues. To break the cycle, someone will have to be big enough to not play the game. That requires love, because it means performing good social behavior with no support from Lisa,** possibly with punishment from her instead.

Lisa herself might grow up enough to be the "someone" who will break the cycle someday. However, in the short run, it's not

**A Check List for Keeping an Eye
on Your Model Disposition:**

1. How many positive remarks do I make to my kids each day?
2. Am I modeling good social skills and tolerance?
3. Do my rules create an atmosphere I enjoy?
4. How many rules can I have and still maintain a pleasant atmosphere?
5. Could I reduce the rules that require policing and enforcement?

likely that anyone will spontaneously change. The most likely adjustment Lisa will make is to "give them back what they give you. If they give you bad behavior, let them taste their own medicine!" Punishment for punishment; silence for silence, or even, silence for punishment (they won't get anything out of me!)

Lisa may extend her use of punishment and later learn to use warnings of punishments to coerce teacher or parent. If demands are not met, she increases the intensity of the demand, and then she tries further punishment—possibly a tantrum. It's coercion. Adults may learn to avoid all this punishment by giving in early. Giving in serves as reward to Lisa, but it also rewards the adults because they successfully avoid Lisa's escalating tantrum.

To break the cycle, someone will have to be big enough to not play the game.

It is a common parent-child relationship where *the child's bad behavior is rewarded* by getting undeserved privileges and avoiding work, and *the parent's "giving in" is rewarded* by successfully avoiding the threat of more bad behavior. It's a case of negative reinforcement (see Chapter 7) for parents and positive reinforcement for Lisa.

In order to have an effect on Lisa, adults need to model a positive disposition for her. It's a big order because that is not what comes to mind and the change is not going to be quick.

Give a Nice Day!

A poor *parental* disposition is almost always the result of a lack of planning about what is important enough to reward and what bad behaviors are trivial enough to ignore.
My experience with six-year-old Harry may be familiar to many parents. Harry came into our office waiting room first and sat on a convenient chair; the mother chose to sit at the opposite side of the seating area. *"Sit over here,"* she said. He moved to the seat next to her. *"Don't swing your foot like that!"* Harry picked up a magazine from the table. *"Be careful with that,"* she said. He turned a page noisily. *"Shh, I told you to be careful!"*

As it turned out, one of the complaints from both teachers and Mom was that *Harry* was bossy and constantly critical of others! Mom had developed an attitude of low expectations and low tolerance and it was contagious. In turn, Harry developed his own habit of being critical of others.

An interesting aspect of a parental disposition such as the one displayed by Harry's mother is that generally a parent uses it only with the child. Parents do not ordinarily act in this punitive way with adults. Rather, they come to expect something different from children and nag about the slightest deviation from the expectations even though the expectations themselves have never been thoughtfully worked out!

What at first appears to be a high standard of behavior by Harry's mother turns out to be actually no specific standard at all. So a parent in such a situation punishes nearly everything and finds no opportunity to reward good behavior.

One teacher I talked to was surprised that Harry was having problems: *"I know he can be difficult but I have decided to catch him doing well. I focus on finding his good moments and when I find one, I let him know it. I think he knows I'm giving him a chance and that I like him."*

> **What at first appears to be a high standard of behavior by Harry's mother turns out to be actually no specific standard at all.**

Adults expect the same of us, more tolerance, more chances to make amends for mistakes, and we show them a better disposition. What is expected of us, and what we expect, creates the social atmosphere we live in. The adult rule is, *"Don't correct or reprimand until a mistake has been made. Certainly withhold punishment—it creates bad feelings."* Here's one reason the atmosphere is better in the teachers' coffee room than in the hallway.

Another teacher I know said that when she went down the school hallway, she noticed classes reacting to their teachers in ways that were "typical" of each teacher's classes. She was surprised that the students could make such quick adjustments as they went from Math to Art to Gym, creating a recognizable atmosphere in each place.

From a selfish point of view, if you were a teacher, how would you like to spend your day? With people who are modeling adult positive attitudes or people who are modeling a punishing disposition?

So how shall we encourage? **No doubt the most effective reward we use is verbal praise and encouragement.** An additional improvement comes when the attitude is imitated. Some parents and teachers may devalue the effect of their attention because they observe only an immediate target behavior. In the longer view, however, a child's disposition will become a close copy of the surrounding adult attitudes.

Give a nice day.

Routine Strategies, Routine Results

The problem illustrated by Harry's mother waiting for counseling is almost always the result of a lack of planning and attention to parental reactions. The critical part of planning that is left out is determining which behaviors are important and which are trivial (see Exercises 2 and 3).

Had Mom ever thought about whether Harry should always sit next to her? She said she had not. Why had she corrected him to do so? She said she was afraid he *"might do something wrong over there."* She said she had no specific fear he would do anything wrong, she just didn't trust him. Some boys might deserve such distrust, but for Harry it was just habit with a little reprimand thrown in. **A psychological leash had been put on, and it was jerked regularly.**

To break the habit of the psychological leash a good rule to include in strategies is, **"Don't correct or instruct your child until you are certain a mistake is being made."** This is the rule that all adults expect you to apply to them, and your children deserve the same treatment until they prove otherwise. Mom (and Dad) should train herself to hesitate before reprimanding, correcting or discouraging a behavior that is not worth the bad feeling.

When Harry's mom tried the "catch 'em being good" suggestion, she told Harry how well he was doing on a part of his homework and, another time, how well he had cleaned up his room. He said, *"What's the matter with you?"*

During the second week, after a few more compliments, Harry's reaction could melt your heart. *"Do you like me?"* he asked. Mom said, *"Of course, I do."* And Harry said, *"Wow."*

The psychological leash is worth breaking for additional reasons. Corrections that are intended as reprimands may become rewards over a long time. They replace the child's responsibility. He just does what he wants while he depends on his parent to make all the corrections. **So while striving for perfection, total dependence is achieved!**

And, to keep it all going, the corrections may come to function as rewards because they are attention. In addition, a disposition is still being learned, of course, and the child may learn the habit of nagging as well. He or she may bring up certain questions continually and harp on them often:

> Caroline: *"But Mommy, why <u>can't</u> I walk to the movies alone?"*
>
> Mom: *"I already told you why, Caroline."*
>
> Caroline: *"I know, but can't I, pleeease!"*
>
> Mom: *"No."*

The next day it starts all over again:

> Caroline: *"Mommy, Mary wants me to walk to the movies with her. Can I go?"*

What events maintain Caroline's nagging? It's a topic that always brings disagreement and punishment, but she continues to bring it up.

The first and most likely reason for this running battle is that Mom and Dad have never held a brief planning session about the problem. Without this strategy session, the reasons given to Caroline change from time to time; her parents disagree from time to time; and they lose confidence in these decisions. The inconsistency encourages Caroline to keep trying because one day she thinks she might hit the right combination of attitudes and get to go. She probably will.

The planning session would nail down the reasons, pinpoint the agreement between Caroline's parents and give them confidence. It would help by stating the honest reasons for the decisions in detail.

Mom: *"Your father and I have decided you can't walk to the movies alone. We think bigger people might make trouble for you along the way and while you're there. When you are ten you may do it. Right, David?"*

Dad: *"Right."*

> *Inconsistency encourages Caroline to keep trying.*

Now will she stop nagging? Probably not, but the amount of nagging will decrease, and Caroline will be a little happier because the situation is now clear, honest, and fair—at least Caroline's parents think so and it gives them confidence. For Caroline, the structure makes the situation more comfortable than the continual argument, although it's still not what she wants. Caroline's argumentive behavior will mellow because the statement of the rule is concrete and detailed—not much room for loopholes.

As the air clears, Caroline's parents need to stay alert and make a special effort to engage and encourage her. They don't want this vacuum to fill with some other unwanted attention-getting behavior. A good disposition, begins with imitation. And it is maintained by experience with reliable rules that produce opportunities to support good social and emotional habits.

Parents need not be forced into the unpleasant task of looking only for the bad mistakes and administering the reprimands or punishments. This is not good for either the parent's or the child's morale. By reducing the overall amount of behavior, it also reduces risk-taking by the child and, therefore, reduces learning.

> *It is often the good behavior that is reduced by frequent punishment.*

In this way, two general characteristics of love, friendship and a good relationship are violated: the child is not given the benefit of the doubt and the child's growth is kept in check by the threat. As Chapter 8 will show, **it is often the <u>good behavior</u> that is reduced by frequent punishment—even mild punishment.** Chapter 9 will take up many alternatives to punishment that adults can live with and children should be blessed with.

Included under punishment is much more than physical punishment. Reprimands, scoldings, and sarcastic comments designed to reduce bad behavior in children are included along with many "left-handed" compliments, punishments disguised as rewards: *"That's certainly a big improvement over yesterday!"* or *"That's very good considering..."*

These statements with double meanings should be watched carefully. Children are less capable of sorting out the subtle meaning and are likely to only get the overall message that they are *still wrong*.

When a child is right, send a clear, positive message without complicated verbal decorations.

5
Daily Messages with Long-Term Effects

Each of us has a few expectations as parents and the messages our rules send show the assumptions we make about our children. A rule change can send the message, *"You are growing up,"* or *"You are still just a child!"* That's one reason many rules don't sit well with adults.

Setting and changing rules need to be done carefully to avoid sending the wrong message. With too many rules the message will be negative, and you may feel you only police your children. But without some short-term rules, moment-to-moment reactions go off in scattered directions seeking one goal and then another. Still, the long-term goal is to get rid of the rules.

The next section will take up the pros and cons of many types of rules. In preparation, this chapter and the following exercise will help you review the goals in your rules and the messages they send to your children.

The goals and rules should not be dramatic ones; they should be guidelines for every day. **Bold messages that suddenly "get through to" a child are seldom accomplished.** What your child comes to expect as a result of consistent experiences will shape the long-lasting patterns.

How Will Others Treat Your Children?

Most people will not treat your children any better than you do! You set the tone for your friends and relatives on how you want your children treated. They are likely to take that message and give your children the same respect and have the same expectations as you.

These other adults will also react to the collection of skills, presumptions, and attitudes your children have acquired *from* you. In your childhood, your expectations included your parents' attitudes that help set your self-concept. Now you are passing that collection to your children—modified by the valuable experience you are willing to add.

> *Most people will not treat your children any better than you do!*

As you pass along your self-concept and your assumptions about your children, they will develop an expectation about how *others* will perceive them. This becomes a self-fulfilling expectation because they take with them a whole pattern of attitudes, assumptions, and habits that will tend to *re*create, in their new social lives, the same social experiences they left behind.

Most people won't treat your children any *worse* than you do, either! People model each other and their reactions tend to create their surroundings. **Each of us causes some people to fade away and others to draw closer. We feather our own social nest.**

Children will pick up your model of how you treat each person. They will pick up your attitude, disposition, and the nature of your appetite for life. Then they are off to recreate their own social environment by reacting to those around them, presenting a certain model, and selecting, without much attention, people who confirm their expectations.

The hard work of parenting is to "handle" the children and influence their habits, but the responsibility is all the more awesome because parents also teach children what to expect *of themselves* and what to expect from others. **So your children learn from your social style and the life philosophy it represents. They learn by imitation and by the way you handle problems in the family *and* they also learn an attitude toward themselves.**

Using the Labels from Theories and Explanations

For many years child psychologists have searched for solutions to the problems of parenthood. Their searches have usually focused on the reasons children do the things they do—in their reactions to parents, to siblings and friends, and to school. If we only knew the reasons, we would know what to do. The solutions would make life easier and we could enjoy parenting more.

But solutions have been difficult to come by because they seem buried in a maze of complicated questions concerning the genes children inherit, the importance of early experiences they have had, and the recent treatment they have encountered from parents and others.

Theories may vividly describe a possible explanation of child behavior and may help you understand the situation. That will be helpful in choosing a reaction in a calm and loving way. However, the purpose of this book is to go beyond theories to applications and help parents find *practical* strategies for action at the moments when problems come up.

Parents cannot afford the common craziness of doing the same thing over and over and expecting to produce a magical

new result! Instead, we could try a new reaction to, for example, a child's anger based on an analysis of the events that make it happen and the reactions that a child gets for "being angry." That is, what happens next? **To enjoy successful parenting, the search for solutions should always return to the question, "What happens next?"**

Searching the possible consequences for explanations allows us to discover how to use our reactions to a child's emotions. The more recognizable the emotion is, the more consistent the reactions to it can be and therefore the more consistent the child's experience and learning. For example, parents can easily agree on when their child is attempting a non-emotional activity, say, walking, and so they know when to help. A description here is easy (whenever she stands up and moves her feet around). Parents usually agree on when to encourage the walker and she learns the task quickly.

Parents often disagree, however, about whether a child is angry, wants attention, or is tired. Often, even one parent cannot decide how to interpret these emotions. How do you react to a moody child who seems "angry" if he might be "tired?" If a father wants the homework done he might decide that an angry child is really just a procrastinating child. A mother trying to get a child off to bed might decide that "angry" is really "tired."

> Dad: *"Allen sure gives us a lot of trouble at dinner."*
>
> Mom: *"It's just that he's tired."*
>
> Dad: *"He's set on ruining it for everyone, I think."*
>
> Mom: *"It's a bad age."*
>
> Dad: *"Well, bad age or not, I'm tired of it."*
>
> Mom: *"What do you want to do, have him eat by himself?"*
>
> Dad: *"No, but we should do something. I'm willing to have dinner a little earlier, if that will help, but I*

*think if he messes up his food, we should take it
away and give him just the one thing he's eating.
If he's not eating anything, we should take it all
away and tell him to ask if he wants anything.
What do you think?"*

Mom: *"OK, but I think our rule should include his
yelling and trying to get down as well as messing
up his food. And I think after we take the food
away we should wait, say two minutes, before we
give him the one food he has been eating, if there
is one."*

Dad: *"OK, let's try it, at least we'll both be using the
same rule."*

Setting Out Long-Term Goals

A parent's short-term job is child-rearing, but the long-term
goal is adult-rearing. To reach that goal, children need examples
of how adults handle their responsibilities and accomplish their
tasks. But kids are not adults yet, and left to their own inclinations,
they may miss their chances to learn. They need a lot of time just
following along while the adults show them the ways of the world.

Given choices, children may lean toward the wrong answers to
questions about how to spend their time: *"What should we do
today?"* *"Do you want to go shopping for the food?"* *"Would you
rather watch TV or help me change the baby's diaper?"*

Asking a child to lead too many family activities risks losing
the adult example and teaching. The skills missed leave a void
where a feeling of pride and usefulness should be developing.
Protected from this education they will feel less useful and less
valuable.

Of course, all members of the family need to have some times when they have it their way. But the productive learning is more likely when the adults do the leading. In *The Gesell Institute's Child Behavior* you are advised to *"try to provide, so far as you can, the kind of situation in which each kind of child can feel comfortable and can do well. But don't try to change him or make him over."* The advice is good except you are not yet told what the "kind of situation" is. The best situations will be ones where children learn by adult example and adult instruction.

The advice from the Gesell book includes a caution to avoid trying to make your child over. It's a little confusing since we are working for some change. So just how far can we go and not be accused of "making him over?"

The way in which a child grows into the independence and competency of adulthood varies from family to family and we all know that the extent of success varies also. **We could probably agree that, ideally, child-rearing should be a process of gradually expanding responsibility and independence.**

Unfortunately, we have all seen many families where the children go through a long period of severe limits followed by an abrupt and risky freedom at about the age of 17 or 18 when the American teenager is sprung from the nest to go to college or work.

Mom:	*"I need some help with dinner every night. Neal, could you set the table for everyone each night?"*
Neal (age 5):	*"Do I hafta? Make Dawn do it."*
Mom:	*"No. Since she turned 9, Dawn makes the whole dinner on Tuesdays and Saturday lunch. You just set the table."*
Neal:	*"I'd rather make a meal like Dawn."*
Mom:	*"OK. Let's work on a few meals together,*

> *maybe we could start tomorrow night. But for now, set the table. That will be a great help!"*

I am sure Neal isn't completely happy with this new chore, but with the proper appreciation, he will have an additional feeling of worth and ability. Dawn is learning she can take care of herself and the family and Neal needs to learn the same.

While living at home, many children experience very little practice with real life responsibilities. Once away from home our offspring-now-sprung will have to learn quickly about getting along with people who are not loving parents, about how to make meals, make car payments, the pitfalls of credit cards and checking accounts, and about leaving time to enjoy life, but not too much time. We had better get started now teaching some of the complications of life.

Most children-turned-teenagers grow up late, painfully, and abruptly, but they grow up. Unfortunately, the newspapers tell us about many young adults who do not cope well with their sudden plunge into independence. As a result, many "children" come back home to live a few more years in the nest—not always a welcome idea to parents.

Mom: *"Neal"* (age 12, now), *"maybe you could balance the checkbook each month this summer."*

Neal: *"What? I don't know anything about that!"*

Mom: *"Well, now's the time to learn. Maybe you should earn a service charge for the job."*

Neal: *"I'll try. But don't get mad if I get it wrong."*

Neal will never ask why he needs to learn decimals in school. He already knows. Coping well with the demands of

**bank accounts, budget management, and the need to plan a
future beyond the end of the month requires a great deal of
practice at the younger ages.**

While parents usually talk to their offspring about the demands
of the outside world, it is easy to forget to allow practice with as
much reality as possible. As soon as reasonable, children need
experience with the freedom to make decisions on their own and
reap the consequences of those decisions. **When they are
successful, the protection of the family nest can make sure that
the success is recognized and encouraged. The failures can be
learning experiences with the consequences softened by the
parents. A long period of safe trial and error is possible for
children whose parents allow for it.**

For Parents, Can "Doing Nothing" Be a Good Idea?

If Jimmy (age 3) has tantrums and Mom lets Jimmy cry it out,
she may find the course unusually difficult for the first few
tantrums. Jimmy feels he needs more attention and continues to
look for ways to get it. Withholding attention from the tantrums
puts more pressure on Jimmy to find another way to his portion of
consideration. Without more planning by Mom and Dad, Jimmy
will find attention harder to come by—a circumstance that
produced the problem in the first place.

Kim was a fourth-grader who took up to four hours each night
to complete the small amount of homework she was assigned. It
was usually about a half-hour's work, but Kim continually
prolonged her work. She had to get another pencil, go to the bathroom again (trip number three), get another paper, start over, etc.

To understand the problem, the question, *"Why?"* has to again
be changed to, *"What happens next?"* What result does Kim get

for losing her place, and then finding her place or deciding to start over because of a small smudge on the paper? It's tempting to say she's particular or a perfectionist, and that might be true. But **before we decide that the problem is inside Kim, let's look at the results of her procrastination, not at school, but right there where it happens.**

The immediate result for Kim turned out to be the prolonged attention of an exasperated mother intent on Kim finishing the work. When I asked, *"What would happen if Kim suddenly finished quickly?"* Mom said, *"That's happened! And I had dinner ready on time that night!"* If Kim did her work efficiently, Mom was gone in a flash to the kitchen. But if homework took a long time, Mom stayed around.

The solution to Kim's problem may seem easy at first. Just do nothing—remove attention for all this procrastination. But Kim is working (or performing "non-working") for Mom's attention, and it would be wrong to ignore that need and "do nothing." Kim needs an acceptable way to be heard, attended, and considered in the family.

So the discovery that Kim is procrastinating for Mom's attention required more than a plan for restricting Mom's attention for this. Mom's new strategy was to give Kim help from 4:00 to 4:30 each afternoon for homework, then Mom did other things. After dinner, time was reserved for Kim to talk with Mom or Dad and do other activities but not homework.

At first, there were problems because Kim was still on home-work after dinner, but after a week the family evenings had improved. Homework time dropped from four inefficient hours to 45 minutes of productive work. In addition, Mom remained alert to other possible activities by Kim that deserved more attention. Kim started helping with dinner and Mom showed her appreciation. Merely removing attention from Kim was not the aim of the strategy. The "do nothing" strategy was actually a plan to look for *more* possibilities for attention to Kim. Completion of homework was still on the list but help with dinner and other evening activities made up a more balanced and healthier list.

For Children, "Do Nothing" Is Not a Good Idea

It's the child's view of the adequacy of attention that determines the need for it. **Parents may feel they give adequate attention and may be correct by objective standards. The child may still feel a need because of the nature of the attention or the timing of it, or because of what he or she has to do to get it.**
Beyond the need for attention, the need for general activity is another condition that is even harder to recognize and more troublesome. "Doing nothing" usually leads to being a little depressed. A child at loose ends does not easily know how to entertain himself, and parents often think he will naturally find what he wants to do if he's told, *"Go find something to do."*

Jerry (7 years old):   *"What a boring day!"*
Dad: *"Lousy weather."* (See Chapter 10 about listening.)
Jerry: *"Yeah. It's too cold to do anything outside."*
Dad: *"Let's draw a plan of the garden."*
Jerry: *"We don't need a plan now, that's way off."*
Dad: *"We could split it up, and you can have a part for your own. Like this ..."*

Jerry's ability to busy himself got a little help from Dad today. He's not happy and bubbly about it, but the boredom will give way because Dad not only has an activity but he is letting Jerry into it as an independent partner. Jerry now has part of the garden.

Grumpy, bored, or depressed children can often improve if only they have a place to spend some energy. Adults learn this remedy for the blues—exercise, chores, and projects help a great deal.

Children often feel only an exciting and new activity will help—something wild like the experiences they see on TV. Most of us adults know that the remedy for boredom doesn't have to be that wild, and it's a good thing, since the "wild things" are rare. Dad will have to illustrate this advice many times as Jerry picks up the habit.

Reactions to Not Enough Attention

A hit-or-miss approach to entertainment has additional problems beyond depression. **There's nothing more dangerous than human beings with too much time on their hands.** All kings, dictators, army officers, college presidents, and teachers learn this principle early or suffer the consequences. So again planning incentives for productive activity is needed.

> **Assigned chores provide something to do, something to be appreciated for, something to be proud of, and something that is a source of self-esteem.**

If some structuring is not provided for the child who is at loose ends, he will cast about and over the undirected years come up with undesirable habits. How a child can entertain himself may be hard to discover if he has no responsibilities to fulfill, no opportunity for useful activity, and no reason to expect any benefit from his choices.

The search here is for a child's opportunities. It's not

necessary to see that she always has something to do. Everyone needs a break and has their own pace of living. But ongoing responsibilities should be available for even the younger children. Assigned chores, for example, provide something to do, something to be appreciated for, something to be proud of, and something that is a source of self-esteem. Some chores can be assigned (and rewarded) without specifying exactly when they are to be done. **If you have a few jobs that you can do when the mood hits you, then that sudden urge for activity has somewhere to go and may occasionally be productive.**

Cleaning a room, practicing a musical instrument, vacuuming, working in the yard, and doing long-term homework assignments need support for their own sake as activity—not just for the result.

So parental support even for the unfinished project is important. If possible, give a few selections of exact times to the child and leave the nagging and badgering out.

The Pursuit of Perfection

Why do children frequently start projects that later falter? Why would a daughter procrastinate on practicing her music when she was so excited at first? Why would she keep missing practice by letting the hours go by? It may be time to increase support for smaller steps. Or you could be content with a less than perfect dedication to the project rather than risk giving attention to the procrastination.

If the goal of music lessons is enjoyment of music, then the little steps along the way are the ones to encourage. The pursuit of perfection was never the purpose. Has her understanding of music increased? It's hard to know. All one can do is support the activity and set a good example through interest. Since progress toward a television debut is not the point, why not just join in her interest and forget perfection? You may be accomplishing more than your children would like to admit.

Sandra:	*"These art museums are boring."*
Mom:	*"Some of these paintings are very famous and very beautiful."*
Sandra:	*"They're all <u>old</u> pictures of <u>old</u> people."*
Mom:	*"But look at this one. Can you see how the artist used light and dark to show how the light comes from the candle?"*
Sandra:	*"I could do that."*
Mom:	*"And look at this one. Look at how some things are made to look far away."*
Sandra:	*"They're just smaller."*
Mom:	*"But they are just the right sizes, and a little less clear."*
Sandra:	*"I guess."*

Is Sandra getting a new appreciation of art? Perhaps not, but be careful in concluding that Sandra's museum trip is a waste of time just because of her attitude. **Remember, sometimes children feel an obligation to make you believe you are not having an effect!** Later on, when she encounters other art or tries out her own painting skills again, you may get a better indication of the usefulness of the museum trip. **Keep your spirits up on the museum trip and guard against following your child into a gloomy attitude. More may be getting done than either of you realize.**

Regardless of your approach to museum trips or child-rearing in general, the question of whether anything has changed in the mind of the child will remain partially unanswered. All parental efforts will seem only partly successful. The children, needing proof they are persons in their own right, want it that way!

Cures and Changes

The idea of a cure implies that some general change has taken place in the individual. But in the approach here, parents consider a priority list of problems, and, behavior chart by behavior chart, focus on one or two problems, plan reactions, and carry them out. For everything else going on, they have to rely on their reflex reactions and the reactions of others. The general cure will have to come from an accumulation of small changes.

> *Changes in child-rearing rarely happen in that quick and easy way. There are no magic pills.*

When we visit the doctor, we all hope for a quick and effortless cure, a magic bottle with pills that are easy to take. Changes in child-rearing rarely happen in that quick and easy way. **There are no magic pills.** There's only you and your child and what your child does, how you react and, later, how the rest of the world reacts.

The strategies described in this book focus on individual problems. The changes brought about by these strategies may be relatively permanent, and that permanence can be somewhat ensured by supporting reactions that you know are likely to be supported by others. Your effort should focus on small problems and emphasize the consistency of consequences.

Exercise and Summary of T-2
TRANSMIT the Right Messages

A. Create a priority list of wanted and unwanted behaviors of your child.

Most of us find it easy to list the potential bad activities of our children and find it hard to think of the good ones. And the list of the bad tends to be more specific than the descriptions of good. "Don't go in the street" is specific enough to draw consequences when the child goes in the street. "Play safe" is too vague to draw much attention when the child does it. Here is a sample worksheet by parents sorting out wanted and unwanted behaviors.

Example: Wanted and Unwanted Behaviors

Good Behaviors to Look For	Possible Good Parent Reactions
Plays w/sister	Comment on their projects together
Homework before dinner	Review homework
Shares TV program choices	Show him I noticed
Helps w/dishes	Sing songs, ask about his day

Bad Behaviors to Discourage	Possible Good Parent Reactions
Yelling in car	Avoid yelling at him; put him alone in back following count-out
Teasing sister	Use count-out, then separate them
Getting upset about homework	Consider positive incentives for starting early
Taking too long to dress	Try to ignore it, then use count-out

** Keep this list handy for sessions when one of these behaviors will be the subject of a new "behavior chart" from the Exercises of Part 1.

B. What priorities would you give to your lists of wanted and unwanted behaviors?

Viewed at the moment of aggravation, a child can seem to have acquired an unbearable habit. Writing down the complaint and prioritizing it often produces a more objective description which may help you understand the problem better even before a planning session begins.

Try to include a behavior chart from the exercise of T-1 (page 28) if you want to have a planning session about the problem. Does the problem usually happen when siblings are around, just before dinner or bedtime, or only when things are a bit boring? A little searching for the conditions may give you new ideas about the reasons for the problem.

What other behaviors of your child also seem to be a problem? We don't want to take on everything at once, but diverting your attention to other problems for a moment is helpful in deciding just how this complaint ranks in the larger picture.

When the broad view is considered, the complaint might not get at the real problem and you might want to restate it. The complaint might be too trivial to worry about now. It doesn't have to be the most important problem in the family, but if it ends up too far down your list of important problems, you might want to choose a better priority.

Rejecting a problem as too unimportant is not wasted time. Some positive action can come of this discovery because often the initial problem was getting attention, reprimands, or nagging. Before moving on to other problems, consider inhibiting *all* corrections and comments for this lowly problem. There is always the risk that part of the reason it exists at all is the attention it gets, and anyway the family airways can always use a little cleaning up to make room for more pleasant times. Now the behavior should cause you less irritation because you have put it in its place.

Example: Defining Priorities

Priority	Desired behavior	Priority	Unwanted Behavior
1	Get homework done	1	Bad to his sister
2	Leave sister alone	2	Throw fit over doing homework
3	Do something besides watch TV	3	Starts screaming
4	Help with dishes	4	Refuses to help around the house
5	Go out and exercise	5	Watches too much TV
		6	Won't keep his shoes on

C. Create a Detailed Description of Your Child's Disposition.

Another area of complaint might be the child's grumpy disposition. In the list from Part A, what priority would you give to this annoyance, and, with this priority, what should be your reaction?

How would you describe your child's disposition? Give the evidence. Pretend we are in court. What objective reasons would you give, that the judge would accept, to support your statement that your child is say, "happy" or "moody?" See the example on the next page.

Example: Disposition Behaviors

He's happy when:	My usual reaction:	He's "in a mood" if:	My usual reaction:
Sings to himself	Usually nothing	Torments sister	Separate them
Pleasant to me	Talk to him more	Refuses everything	Argue and demand
Is cooperative	Accept his help	Won't answer until threatened	Threaten

T - 3
TAKE ON
Just a Few Good Rules

Rules for children should teach useful
capabilities so that they will know, as soon as
they can, that they are growing more capable.
After that, they need encouragement to use
their capabilities in their own individual ways.

> *"Children are not vessels to be filled,*
> *but candles to be lit."*
> —Sophia Lyons Fahs

6
Planning Sessions for
a Few Good Rules

Parents need time for planning child-rearing strategies. This may sound devious and scheming, but remember how much time and energy your children have for working things out their way. Even though they may not be aware of their own intentions, they react, adjust and react again. With the advantage of time available for planning and trying out solutions over and over, children can gain too much control of the family activity. **Occasional planning sessions can keep the balance and fairness in family relationships.**

Holding to Reasonable Rules

Very young children don't usually show strong resistance to the parents' rules because they find natural gratification in many of the behaviors required. While growing from one to five, it's automatically gratifying to succeed in dressing yourself, tying your own shoe, or in overpowering and using a spoon. **In these cases, the obvious usefulness of the task is a great advantage to the teaching parent.**

> *Working out a justification can be more than a defense, it can be a review that will lead to eliminating rules no longer needed.*

But how quickly the obvious worth of the task becomes debatable. After mastering the spoon, the next lesson is table manners. After successful dressing, the next lesson is proper selection and care of clothes. Now the parents must examine the reasoning behind their rules and they are challenged to defend them. Arbitrary requests can put parents in the uncomfortable position of defending *their own* values. It's a small argument with a small person, but it is an ominous preview of the confrontations to come in the next 15 to 20 years.

Of course, all parents from time to time neglect working out the reasons for the requests they make of their children. When surprised, they find themselves rationalizing in a desperate attempt to protect their authority and quell a childish rebellion. **Working out a justification can be more than a defense, it can be a review that will lead to eliminating rules no longer needed.** Out of habit a parent may continue to react and control behavior in an area where independence should replace inconvenient and unpleasant control.

Sometimes when a child is given a chore, a procrastination game can develop to provoke attention. Parents may nag, plead, and prod the child to do a chore, all the time worrying that the "game" is being prolonged for the child's entertainment.

When parents feel reduced to unpleasant nagging, they may be tempted to blame the child not only for failure in the task, but for making them unhappy with the task of nagging.

It's time to pause for a parent conference to look for a new strategy. Some of the following conclusions and strategies might be good starting points for such conferences.

Possible Alternatives to Consider in the Planning Session

1. **The behavior is too trivial to bother with.** Let's ignore it and eliminate a lot of unpleasant nagging and make more time for other kinds of conversation. This might apply to the way a child combs his/her hair, posture while watching TV or the few scraps of food always left on the dinner plate.

2. **The justification is off in the future.** When she/he starts noticing the impression others get from messy hair, sloppy posture, or wasteful habits, then we'll see a change. Let's wait for the expansion of his/her social circle to do it. Right now we can avoid a sacrifice of our family atmosphere by ignoring the "problem."

3. **The behavior is worth changing.** Let's think up a consequence that could work and stop all the nagging. From now on, anyone in the family showing terrible posture or wasting food has to put a penny in a jar on the kitchen table. Anyone completing a day without having to put in a penny may take ten cents from the jar (Mom or Dad pay off if the jar is empty).

4. **The behavior is worth changing, and it hasn't changed because the kids know they're getting through to us.** A reward is already working—it's the very nagging and pleading

that we thought would solve the problem! It's time to pay close attention to ignoring this bad habit and looking for any time we can encourage little glimmers of good behavior that we hope will replace it.

Mom:	*"Let's all be in the clean plate club tonight!"*
Carlos:	*"I hate green stuff."*
Maria:	*"Me too!"*
Mom:	*"It's all good for you. Now eat up. I try hard to ..."*
Maria:	*"I'll take one bite."* (Spoons up just enough to show up on a laboratory slide.)
Mom:	*"You too, Carlos."*
Carlos:	*"This is ridiculous."*
Mom:	*"Now Carlos, we have cookies for dessert."*
Carlos:	*"I don't even like cookies."*
Mom:	*"You know you like cookies ..."*

Later, in the planning session blame sets in:

Dad:	*"That was a good dinner, but eating it was miserable!"*
Mom:	*"Well, that's the way kids are, you know. I can't force them to eat."*
Dad:	*"Carlos just does it to argue, and then they both eat what they want later. It's an attention-getting thing."*
Mom:	*"It's their way of getting into the conversation."*
Dad:	*"Maybe we should eat later, alone."*
Mom:	*"That's a solution for us, but that won't make them eat any better. How about this idea: if you back me up on "no snacks," I'll just put out*

what we all should eat and that's it! They won't starve, they'll eat some of it, and maybe we can talk about something besides food at dinner."

Dad: *"They'll whine for other stuff. We'll just have to ignore that."*

Mom: *"We tell them once that this is what we are having for dinner—that's it. I just won't have cookies and other stuff in the house. It won't always be convenient, but it's better than all this fighting to get them to eat."*

Dad: *"Carlos will gripe all the way through dinner."*

Mom: *"We just have to bring up other topics like we would with visitors. He'll gripe at first but if we stick to it, he'll get used to eating what he wants of what is there. Just don't buy into the 'I'll-bet-you-can't-make-me-eat' game."*

Dad: *"Me!? You're the one who ..."*

Mom: *"OK, OK. Never mind that, we have to be together on this. Remember we agreed to support each other in these sessions, not to go after each other."*

Dad: *"OK, let's try it. As long as they're healthy, let them pick what they want from what we serve."*

Mom: *"We can even have a little dessert; just remember to bring in other subjects that they can be in on."*

Dad: *"And if it doesn't work, we can always have another session."*

The strategy planned here may need modification later, and Mom and Dad will certainly need another session on other problems. **The advantage of the session is that Mom and**

Dad are trying out a new way of handling a problem—not just reacting to each moment as it comes up—and, they feel *they* are in control of what's going on.

5. **The behavior is worth changing, not so much for reasons that benefit the child but because we would find it more pleasant and comfortable that way.** It's not for the child's sake but for ours that we start the penny-jar procedure or the plan to ignore the bad behavior or the goal of looking for the good behavior to encourage. This may seem selfish but it can be valid. **There's a time for selfishness in parenting:**

> Jerry: *"Mom, why can't I stay out late and play every night? How can I get hurt in my own yard on some nights and not others? It doesn't make sense!"*
>
> Mom: *"Well, on most of those nights you need the extra time for homework."*
>
> Jerry: *"If I have my homework done, can I stay out?"*
>
> Mom: *"You also need to rest sometimes."*
>
> Jerry: *"Can I watch TV?"*
>
> Mom: *"Well, I, ah, really meant for you to rest."*

Sometimes the real justification for this kind of rule is that the parents want some evenings when they can have peace of mind and not worry about possible accidents and what's going on out there.

> Mom: *"I want you here with us some nights because I don't want to worry every evening."*

This frank statement of parents' rights might not end the argument, but at least Mom can feel more comfortable knowing she has a fair and above-board position.

Selfishness can be justified occasionally, but dishonesty cannot. Parents should consider their reasons for rules even in the early years when children are only beginning to use rationality as a challenge. If five-year-old Timmy can't go running and screaming through the house because it annoys Dad, telling him it is because nice boys don't do things like that is off target and changes the subject from an action (running) to a person (Timmy).

Without the consideration of Dad part, the message about Dad being annoyed gets mixed up with, *"Dad thinks I'm not nice."* The message sent is now much more than intended. We just wanted him to stop annoying us; he thinks we said he's a bad person.

Avoiding Rules That Only Work Once

Some planned consequences are better than others when it comes to their value in learning. A parental reaction of, *"If you don't stop running through the house all the time, we won't go to the circus,"* or, *"We won't sign you up for soccer this year!"* ignores the principle of repeated *practice*.

Going to the circus is a single future event not likely to be repeated for some time. It's tempting to repeat the threat many times since the circus itself will only happen once. Your child does need to learn that you should be taken seriously and that you mean what you say about the circus or about soccer, but the consequence is so far off that any outcome will seem arbitrary.

> *It's tempting to repeat the threat many times since the circus itself will only happen once.*

So after all the argument, you either take the kid to the circus and admit giving in, or you hold to your threat, don't take her/him to the circus, and admit you are giving no credit for the better behaviors. This says that, overall, he/she has been a bad kid. It's a one-shot consequence with no winners and little chance of a satisfactory outcome.

Another problem with a single consequence is that parents are tempted to do a lot of talking in order to "milk" all the influence they can from the upcoming big event. The temptation is to hold the

> *Allow yourself and your family the enjoyment of individual events without trying to use them to limit bad or produce good behavior.*

possibility of punishment over the child for days or weeks. This situation is gloomy for the family and for the event when it finally comes. It's like holding off the enemy in battle with only one bullet; you have to do a lot of posturing, bluffing, and threatening. Once a parent decides on the circus, she is an ogre for not allowing it or a patsy for giving in! **And then the next day, she will need a new bullet with a new threat.**

A better strategy is to allow yourself and your family the enjoyment of individual events without trying to use them to limit bad or produce good behavior. Instead, choose some smaller event that can come up more frequently, something not so severe, and something that has a positive side to emphasize. For example, instead of threatening to throw away all the toys that you have to pick up (an unmanageable and expensive threat with an "only once" character to it), you could designate a "daily toy closet" where any toys go that are still scattered after Dad has asked for them to be picked up. The closet will be opened only at a certain time and then the toys can be reclaimed by their owners. Any toy left for parents to pick up after that is put in the closet for the next opening.

This procedure has the advantage of being a consistent and repeatable consequence. It is not so severe as to make parents feel guilty and inconsistent, and it is logically related to the problem of too much mess or danger from toys being left out.

A repeatable consequence makes it much easier to refrain from nagging. The repetition does the reminding. Nagging can stop, opening the airways for more pleasant family talk.

Definitions for Actions

In order to know when to react, a clear description of the behavior is necessary so that you'll identify it when you see it. If you make a bet concerning which of two children will be first to share a toy with a new child, how will you decide who wins the bet?

This is not like betting on a horse race where everyone knows what a "winner" is—especially now that we have photographs of the finish. A bet on a child's sharing can be a difficult problem in definitions.

We need an objective definition of "sharing" and then agreement on what to look for. Otherwise, there's too much room for interpretation, and the bettors may not always agree. For example, if a child offers one of his toys to another child, that will be called sharing for the purposes of the bet. It is not necessary to know *why* the child shares or what is on the child's mind at the moment. He may share because others are watching or to get a toy from the other child, or for other "wrong" reasons. But a bet's a bet, and if the parents want to support sharing in their child, they will need a similar definition, and they too will not know the child's mind at any moment.

Definitions help parents agree on when encouragement— concrete pay-off or social praise—will be given. This decision is important. If parents agree on what the good behavior is, then it becomes the signal for parental attention.

In addition to making things clear, well-defined rules about what is right also give the child the advantage of quickly understanding what *to do*. **If frequent little talks and explanations seem necessary, the definition itself, or the reaction to it, may be too vague or variable.**

> *A reprimand or correction always runs the risk of being more effective as attention than as the negative it was intended to be.*

The goal here is consistent, repeated practice with a reasonable, and very obvious, consequence.

For the purpose of the bet, the behavioral definition of sharing was one child offering a toy to another. When the child drifts away from sharing by, say, snatching a toy from his playmates, the temptation to correct or reprimand such a "mistake" deserves careful consideration.

A reprimand or correction always runs the risk of being more effective as attention than as the negative it was intended to be. In most cases **ignoring the mistakes and emphasizing the positive is best.** In Chapter 8 and 9 we will take up alternatives to punishment as reactions to errors and mistakes.

How Much Explanation Is Required for Children?

Not all the whys and wherefores concerning a request from a child need prolonged explanations. **Explanations are important when a new rule is to go into effect, but repeated requests for explanations may be just a form of filibustering to get the rule changed or to postpone it. What is important for learning and for reliable and desirable behavior patterns is a consistent relationship between action and parental *reaction*.**

When you learn to drive a car, you don't understand all the complicated mechanisms of the car. An understanding of pistons, cams, and ignition systems is not necessary. As long as the accelerator, brake, steering wheel, and ignition key work consistently, you can learn very well. Learning becomes a nightmare if the car is difficult to start, has inconsistent brakes, or sloppy steering!

In the same way, a child can gain experience from a reliable set of rules and policies without knowing all the adult reasoning behind the rules. Consistency is enough; understanding how the car engine works or why parents are anxious about certain situations may help, but is not required.

It would be a waste of time for driving schools to give detailed courses on internal combustion engines. At some stages, it may be a waste of time to continually tell a child about germs when asking him to wash his hands before eating. An occasional reminder might be useful even at age 3, but repeated explanations may become attention for dirty hands.

A study concerning this need for understanding was conducted by E. R. Guthrie and G. P. Horton in the early years of psychology. In their experiments, a cat was placed in a problem box. As most cat owners know, cats enjoy exploring small spaces, but it is not in a cat's nature to be content in a confined place. A pole in the center of the box could open the door *if* the cat pushed it, but because the cat didn't know about the pole, it tried various actions to escape. It mewed and scratched at first, and then as it paced around, it bumped the pole and gained its freedom. This was not an insight any more than a child's first use of a doorknob is an insight. It was an accident. Nevertheless, a certain behavior did produce a good result, and when the cat was again put in the box, it was a little faster in getting out.

History does not tell us how many scratches Guthrie and

Horton suffered, but they did put the cat into the box several times. The cat escaped faster and faster by rubbing the pole in the way a cat rubs a person's leg, thus releasing the latch. The cat didn't have to learn about latches and springs and hinges. Mechanical engineering is above a cat. It didn't face the pole, grab it or scratch it. It only learned the necessary: stand here, swing your rear so you rub the pole, leave.

Most of the everyday behaviors learned by children are also learned without a complete understanding of the processes involved. **From rattles and noisy toys, to spoons, doorknobs, computers and TV remotes, to pleasing Daddy and Mommy, their skills develop and race far ahead of their understanding.** Children, and adults at times, only understand that certain activities produce good results and often that's enough. So it's best to be brief and conservative with explanations of rules—especially when a son or daughter seems to be enjoying the argument.

Necessary Planning About Strategies

The advantage enjoyed by Guthrie and Horton's cat was that it was placed in a situation where success was likely. The box was not room size and the pole was not broom size. The rule was about a behavior well within the cat's ability. The set-up was good, and the planned consequence, the escape, was ready and delivered quickly. **As a learning strategy, it had all the right ingredients.** The process of specifying how a behavior will result in a planned consequence is the strategy.

Parents who neglect planning enter every child-rearing situation one step behind their children.

The word "strategy," when applied to child-rearing, may at first imply a little too much struggling, a little too much confrontation, or even scheming. And there is a little of each of these in adult-rearing.

The important thing is to devote time and effort to conscious, routine planning. Think about how much time and energy children have for figuring out how to accomplish their goals! Parents who neglect planning enter every child-rearing situation one step behind their children.

When I ask parents in training groups to spend 15 to 30 minutes each week in a strategy session, most parents find it difficult to set aside that time. On the other hand, their children, with no jobs and few domestic responsibilities, have plenty of time for planning tryouts of new ideas and methods on their parents. It is a blessing that children are poor time managers!

> *Think about how much time and energy children have for figuring out how to accomplish their goals!*

Children are not all scheming little devils, but they do constantly test and experience their family situations, like the cat, only with more thought. If parents of a 15-year-old have lost some control over their son or daughter, it might be due to the many hours of the last few years the teenager spent searching for solutions to frustrations compared with the number of hours his or her parents spent thinking through plans for change.

Most parents of "kids gone wrong" are not guilty of bad decisions that led to bad procedures; usually it was that their hectic schedule didn't leave time for planning and the lack of planning was a factor in the outcome.

So the planning session is a necessity. It allows parents to regroup, to compromise in private, and to agree on a united front. It ensures that the behavior of concern will be recognized and consequences will be consistent. It need not be secretive. In most cases, telling your son or daughter the results of the session is beneficial. If a strategy will only work if the children don't know what it is, then it's unlikely to work, is a little dishonest, and it's probably unrealistic because the children will find out.

For single parents, the compromises, the agreement, and the united front may have to take place in one's own mind, but that may be the most important place for consistency anyway. Chapter 15 takes up the advantages of support groups for single parents.

7
Adult Rules for Children?

At every stage of life people need some respect and recognition. It doesn't need to be money. Often praise, encouragement, and admiration will do. But support in some form is crucial for the essential feeling of self-worth. That's a particularly elusive feeling for a child.

It's tempting to think that children growing up from "below" us should be content with good care. But their effort to grow needs strong positive support so that they value themselves and develop self-confidence. What positive support can we have ready for them?

What are Kids Looking For?

"It's amazing how Duncan has taken to helping in the kitchen! He's four and yet he can really do things! He made his own scrambled egg the other morning. I told him how impressed I was, and he made one for me!"

What fun it is to impress your parents! Duncan loves to help

with cooking, doing a little on his own, and having his parents say
how great he is. One counselor I know said the **high point of a
boy's,** *or a grown man's,* **life is when his father tells him he's
the fine son his father hoped to have.** I'm sure it's the same for
daughters and the hope for general approval
from Mom is just as important.

> *The older you are,
> the more reward
> is expected for
> any effort.*

   **Since parental approval is such an
emotional high point, it is a shame some
parents often begrudge their children
"too much" reward.** Reward and
reinforcement are terms that may sound too
mechanical because the words imply a
contrived influence on behavior. But the most frequent reward
children receive is the admiration and appreciation expressed by
parents. Parents who are generous with these "rewards" are more
effective.

   **Yet many are still uncomfortable with the notion that
selfish benefit is required to get children, or anybody else, to do
the right thing.** *"They should do it for the love of it, shouldn't
they? They know it's good for them! They had better be glad they
have a good home and a chance to learn and advance!"* Isn't this
the way we all feel sometimes? Sometimes it seems unbelievable
that kids would pass up an opportunity for personal growth, or fail
to contribute to the family out of appreciation for the care they get.

   It's children we're talking about, of course. Employees who
are asked to work a little longer or teachers asked to carry a larger
load *deserve* rewards for their extra work. And our boss who
expects something for nothing just doesn't understand our personal
economic situation!

   **As a matter of fact, the older you are, the more reward is
expected for any effort**—managers and school principals don't
feel respected unless they make a little more money. Corporate

officers and members of congress worry that lower salaries for them would bring in people less competent than themselves; and CEO's demand golden parachutes of stock options so they will have the "proper incentive" to do a good job up there at the top. So the higher ups commonly get more money *and appreciation* while neither money nor appreciation is common lower down the chain.

However, when thinking about *negative* consequences such as punishment for mistakes, we often include possibilities for those lower down that would be too severe for higher-ups. Some would say punishment is even *necessary* for the little ones.

Debates about punishments, taken up in the next two chapters, have a ring of prejudice to them: *"A little spank would straighten him up!" "That sassy little girl needs a good smack!"* And the prejudice continues in some views of rewards also, *"If you reward children, soon they'll only perform for rewards." "Money will spoil children or make little materialists out of them."* Yet the adults who make these comments would even *change jobs or cities* in order to get more appreciation, status, or money.

> *We often include punishments for those lower down that would be too severe for higher ups.*

Of course, adults rightfully expect appreciation for their contribution, and they expect to go unpunished and given another chance for their mistakes. A good supervisor will recognize that fact and support good adult performance with positive reactions. Children deserve the same.

Everyone Wants to Be Treated Like An Adult

In showing appreciation and respect for children, it is often a good idea to ask what the proper consequence would be if our problem person were an adult. For example, Raymond at age seven continually disrupts dinner with loud, inappropriate noises, giggles, and comments. You might ask, *"What would we do about an adult, say, Uncle George, if he acted this strangely?"*

> *Raymond is not as skilled with language, and it's hard for him to break into the conversation without some adult consideration.*

For Uncle George, you might first try to change the subject and calm him down by bringing up a subject of interest to him. It's an obvious suggestion because we all know that the person most in danger of becoming obnoxious is the one who is left out, bored, or has nothing to do. The conversation should include Uncle George if we want a pleasant and comfortable guest, and perhaps the same goes for little Raymond.

If that didn't work, you might try a reprimand on Uncle George and the same might be used on Raymond. Beyond that, we would probably abandon the positive reinforcement idea, and **our view of the Uncle problem and the Raymond problem would become very different.**

Uncle George would probably be tolerated with a mental note not to have him back. Raymond, on the other hand, would probably be punished, sent to his room perhaps, or even snatched from his chair for a little stern squeeze. That might get results for the short run, but as experienced parents know, the dinner situation would be ruined, everyone would be mad, and Raymond, unlike Uncle George, will be back.

Raymond might do better if he got some adult treatment.

Step One for Raymond might be to have him eat earlier the next evening. Then when he comes back, we might use the Uncle George treatment for Step Two—a conversation at Raymond's level and interest. If there is more trouble we could repeat Step One of having Raymond eat earlier for an evening, and Step Two of having Raymond back for another try. How many times? Probably until Raymond gets it right since we can't just send him off—Uncle George probably won't take him!

Another approach to looking for reasons for Raymond's behavior is to ask, *"If Raymond was not behaving badly, what would be available to him and what would be our reaction?"* Is there any suggestion or incentive for Raymond to show any *particular* behavior? This approach leads us back to the change-the-subject-to-fit solution.

But when Dad and Mom sit down to dinner, they have stories to tell about their day at work and elsewhere. Raymond has stories also, but he's not as skillful with language and **it's hard for him to break in if he doesn't get some patient consideration.** It's difficult for Raymond if Mom reports on a conversation at work and Dad comments on the TV news and Mom responds with her description of the newspaper report on the same story and Dad says...and Mom says...and Raymond gets in the conversation only by acting up.

The adult conversation might only recognize Raymond's presence with, *"Sit up in your chair,"* *"Eat your peas,"* *"Don't make bubbles in your milk,"* and the ever-popular, *"Now look what you've done!"* Which is *exactly* what Raymond wanted everyone to do—look at what he was doing!

Is this how Raymond gets his share of the dinner conversation? Uncle George would chime in on the news report or Mom's work experience, but Raymond is not up to that and so he has to settle for negative attention—better than no attention—and he probably hopes the whole situation will soon be over.

This notion of deserved attention might also apply to a child in a classroom. David's problem comes up in the lulls in classroom activity. **You might say that David, like Raymond, doesn't know enough to busy himself without getting into trouble,** but another way to put it is that, for David, the opportunities for good behavior are not obvious enough for him. If he's a first or second grader you wouldn't expect him to know what to do. **He lacks practice and if the class is large, the rewards for "acting right," even if he knows what that means, are likely to be infrequent and the benefits obscure.**

> *It takes a fine teacher or mother to be able to catch David or Raymond being good and provide the encouragement and attention he needs.*

It takes a fine teacher or mother to be able to catch David or Raymond being good and provide the encouragement and attention he needs. If the teacher can hold to the view that the problem is a *lack* of something in the classroom that David needs, not an unchangeable problem inside David, David can improve just like Raymond.

Use Attention Thoughtfully When the Messages are Important

You don't have to carry around a bag of money and candy to keep the kids shaped up. You carry around yourself and, for the most part, that's enough. An honest expression of appreciation, praise, and encouragement can be very effective *if* done thoughtfully.

Social rewards are so easy to give that they are often given

in an offhand manner—forgotten when they are most needed, thrown in when they send the wrong message. A rigid plan of reactions to your children would not be good either. But a continuous flow of casual attention has the danger of highlighting troublesome behaviors and unimportant activities, making bad behavior out of what was, at first, trivial.

> Mom: *"Careful with the eyes on the teddy bear, they could come off."*
>
> Kayla: *"They could come off?"*
>
> Mom: *"They're just sewn on."*

Kayla starts to finger the eyes of the teddy bear.

> Mom: *"I told you to be careful. Just leave them alone."*
>
> Kayla: *"They won't come off, see?"*
>
> Mom: *"Don't do that! They'll come off."*

Whether Kayla or her mom turn out to be right about the teddy bear, the situation is now a confrontation, and if I were the teddy bear, I'd be nervous. **Mom started fixing a problem before she had one, and now she has one.** Let's have her try another situation:

> Kayla: *"I'm gonna sit on a regular chair tonight."*
>
> Mom: *"OK."*
>
> Kayla: *"Really. I'm big enough."* (Here's a hint that we are into an attention-getting game. Why didn't Kayla just sit when she got the "OK" from Mom?)
>
> Mom: *"Uh huh."*
>
> Kayla: (Sits on a regular chair) *"I can't see from here.* (Waits, gets no reaction) *I want my old chair*

back, but I want it over here."

Mom: "OK. I'll help you move it." (Now Mom reacts
         to a reasonable request.)

Mom's bland reaction to Kayla's first idea provided no spot-light for Kayla's seating problem. She tries something that's not satisfac-tory, and then something that is. All the time Mom does a good job by keeping this demand at the level of importance that it deserves.

Your social rewards, then, deserve close attention at times. You can't police yourself every moment, watching every move of your child and every word you say, and it would be an awful and inhuman situation for anyone who did. But when you are considering a *specific* behavior of your child, always consider the role your social attention plays—for good or ill.

Sophisticated adults give social attention and approval in subtle ways that can send mixed (and mixed up) messages to a child. We use a nod of the head or lift of an eyebrow or a curiously phrased remark such as, *"I guess you finally got that right."* Or, *"All right, you're better than last week." "You bet." "Oh, right, what a great job that was!"*

It's hard to put into print exactly what these remarks mean without a description of inflections and pauses and tone of voice. Adults have a lot of practice in using and hearing such subtleties and react and learn from each of them. But **a child, not yet grown up, hasn't learned all the details of sarcasm or understatement and the meanings these details convey.**

Make sure your sophistication doesn't get in the way when you are trying to support your child. Send your message clearly; be frank and outspoken when you like what has been done: *"Yes, that's good." "That's what I like you to do."* Say it loud enough; say it simply; let him or her know you mean it.

What is "Negative Reinforcement?"

The purpose of regular punishment, as everyone knows, is to reduce or eliminate bad behavior. Chapters 8 and 9 will discuss the pros, cons, and alternatives to that procedure. **Negative reinforcement is not punishment for mistakes; it's punishment for *failing* to do the *right* thing!**

The threat of a consequence for failing to meet someone's expectations is a common experience in a routine day. Why do I make dinner for the kids at the same time every night, use their favorite plate, prepare only certain foods? Is it because they watch for their chance to support my "good" behavior? No, the answer here usually begins, *"Well, if I didn't do that, the kids would complain and make a lot of trouble."*

If it's the *lack* of performance that would produce bad consequences, it's negative reinforcement. As long as I avoid unwanted dinner delays, unwanted food, and do not disappoint my little masters, *I avoid* their nasty behavior. Parents also use negative reinforcement. For example, if the children don't act up and fight, *they can avoid* my mad reaction.

The difference between regular punishment and negative reinforcement is important. Regular punishment in its consistent form is painful but easy to understand: *"If I do the wrong thing, I'll get bad consequences."* Negative reinforcement is also painful, but the rule is more obscure: *"If I fail to do the right thing, I'll get bad consequences."*

Mom:	*"Zac, did you pick up your toys?"*
Zac:	(Watching TV) *"Not yet."*
Mom:	*"Did you put your dirty clothes in the laundry?"*
Zac:	*"No."*
Mom:	*"How about the mess in the living room?"*

Zac: *"OK. As soon as this is over."*

Mom: *"Take those dishes out, too."*

Zac: *"OK."* (Remains an intimate part of the couch.)

Mom: (She's used no punishment up to here, but now she reacts to Zac's *lack* of action.) *"Zac, I have had it! Now turn off that TV and get these things cleaned up!"*

Zac: *"OK, OK. Don't have a cow about it."* (Mumbling) *"Gee, who knows when you're gonna blow up, anyway?"*

Mom: *"What was that?"*

Zac: *"Nothing."*

Part of Zac's and Mom's problem is that Mom's strategy is negative reinforcement. If Zac fails to perform (enough times) and Mom asks him (enough times) then Mom gets mad. Mom may also support and compliment Zac if he cleans things up, but Mom's exasperation limit and Zac's fear of her are the main factors at work in the situation.

At times, the distinction between regular punishment and negative reinforcement may seem like a word game. Could we simply say that Mom threatens regular punishment for Zac's sloppiness? She *could* use that strategy, lock up the toys when she sees them left out, for example. But the punishment she uses is triggered by the *lack* of behaviors and occurs at a non-specific time. Zac is tempted to continue to procrastinate, delay, and test the limits while Mom is driven to using "mad" as a motivator.

Negative reinforcement does not produce a happy situation. If you do most of your activities every day just to avoid someone's flack, you're probably unhappy with him or her (we all know who we mean!).

Dad: *"Did you take the car in today?"*

Mom: *"Yes, it just needed a tune up."*

Dad: *"Great, thanks for getting it over there; that takes a lot off my mind."*

Dad used the positive reinforcement idea, but in the next minute he slips to negative reinforcement:

Dad: *"Did you get the little dinners I wanted for lunches?"*

Mom: *"Didn't go by the store after work."*

Dad: *"Hey, how am I supposed to work all day without lunch?"* (Here's a reprimand as negative reinforcement for Mom's failure to do the right thing.)

Mom: (Borrowing from Zac) *"OK, OK, don't have a cow over it. I'll get them tomorrow and I'll make something good for you to take in the morning."* (Mumbling) *"Gee, beam me up, Scotty!"*

Dad: *"What was that?"*

Mom: *"Oh, nothing."*

Using Incentives

In a more perfect world, everyone would do the right things for the right reasons. We wouldn't need special incentives such as paychecks, bonuses, benefits, or parents using the right reaction. The work would be done because we all know it needs to be done.

But in the real world, all dieters, regular working folks, and exercisers know that free-floating motivation is hard to maintain. We either keep going in order to avoid the negative reinforcement, or some positive reinforcement better be in the offing.

Concrete rewards may also be needed when laziness has become so habitual, and resistance to change so strong that we need contrived rewards to make even small steps in progress. For example, to improve the homework study habit, you might adjust the weekly allowance according to the amount of homework done. Some allowance is coming the child's way anyway, and there is important school work to be done, so the real world might as well start right here—the work and the pay go together.

> *Start at the level of the child now, establish his/her confidence, then the requests can be increased.*

Set the limits, both minimums and maximums, so that you can't be cornered into an unreasonable position such as allowing *no* money if no homework gets done or having to pay too much if all the homework is done. You will want to keep it simple, but without stated limits you'll be tempted to give out undeserved money or have to refuse to pay up for a sudden burst of activity.

It will be better to set limits at the beginning—say a $3.00 minimum and a $10 maximum. The practice is the most important thing going on in the child's life, so let's give practice some importance. We guarantee the minimum by saying, *"The $3.00 is for every week, but I'll add a dollar for each night your homework is all done, and two extra for a whole week of successful homework nights."* You could tie the definition of "homework done" to pages of workbooks, teacher assignments, or time spent on homework each night.

With this amount of structure, you'll avoid being an ogre who won't give any allowance, and you'll avoid extravagant payoffs for bursts of activity. After a few weeks, you may want to add special incentives for some subjects, change the definition of "home-work done," or add an extra pay increase for special efforts. All rules are subject to change.

One of the keys to success in using incentives is to make very reasonable requests, especially at first. Base these requests not on what *should* be done but on what *has been the usual.* An incentive for doing hours of homework for a child who has not been able to stick with it for 10 minutes in the last three months is doomed to failure. Start at the level of the child now, establish his/her confidence, then the requests can be increased.

On day one, you want to guarantee that you will get an opportunity to use your incentive! Plan an incentive for a performance not only within your child's ability but within his/her inclination as well. For example, you might ask that only one page of a workbook assignment be completed before a whole half-hour of TV is approved. The payoff is so attractive and the price tag so small that a success is likely.

With little successes "in the bank," you can start a progression toward the amount of homework required before the reward is available. The increments should be small enough to allow a smooth and easy increase in effort.

> *Even children who moan and complain when asked to pitch in, still grow a little when they do pitch in.*

You must be careful when contriving "materialistic" rewards because they are usually not a natural benefit of the behavior and the time will come when your children will be out on their own and faced with less generous people. This means that your encouragement, admira-tion, and praise must remain a major part of the rules even when using concrete rewards. Your reactions must continue to send the message of the import-ance and usefulness of the activities you support. You hope that your target objectives are likely to be supported outside the family in a way that is at least enough to keep your child on the right path.

The activities that other people support and believe important are probably the same as yours. Chores such as washing the car, mowing the lawn, painting, cooking, and shopping are some of the easy ones. Teens usually value the same activities but it may not be "in" to say so.

The child's habitual attitude toward chores should not mislead parents. Chores are useful in building self-esteem and self-respect. Even children who moan and complain when asked to pitch in, still grow a little when they *do* pitch in. Everyone wants to feel competent and able. **So when you ask your child to do chores, take heart in the fact that the advantage goes far beyond getting the chores done. As a matter of fact, the boost in the child's self-respect may be the most important outcome!**

Now as you allow your offspring into adult activities, remember to include the fun as well as the less desirable parts of the job. When washing the car, she should get to use the hose as well as scrub the wheels. When shopping for food, he should be allowed to pick out a goody as well as get the soap.

One last caution concerning the first efforts to support good behavior: the proof of a little success is in the daily and weekly changes, *not* the immediate reactions of the kids. Remember kids can be very pessimistic about your power. The pessimism may come from their own feeling of powerlessness as well as a desire to discourage you from trying to influence them! Don't buy it. The proof of change is in the longer term reactions and adjustment.

A second related tactic of your kids may be to belittle the consequence as too weak to do any good. The power of consequences is in their accumulated numbers. Small compliments and encouragement, *"You're running the laundry through by yourself? You really are growing up!"* or *"Gerry, why don't you call in the pizza order, you're getting so good on the phone."*

Every penny in the bank adds up—don't be talked out of it, just say (or think), *"Let's see how it goes."*

8

Ten Reasons "Get Tough" Punishment Seldom Works

> When a puppy goes on the rug, it's tempting to swat him, but he doesn't learn much from that. And tomorrow it will be harder to teach him *anything* because he will be a little more timid—and harder to find!

"You're too easy on the kids! Let me have them for a week. They'll shape up after a couple of swats from their Uncle Harry!"

Nancy and Martin, seven and eight years old, can be real trouble as a sister-brother team in a game of "Let's-see-how-much-we-can-get-away-with." They act up or throw tantrums for attention or they tease and fight with each other just for entertainment. Any suggestion to Nancy or Martin by their parents that they do "something nice" is rejected, perhaps because that would mean the game would be over.

Most of the relatives, including Uncle Harry, think that stern talk and a few extra swats would fix the "Nancy-and-Martin" problem. They think they would somehow use punishment more effectively and more consistently than Nancy and Martin's parents, but they're on the wrong track for several reasons.

Reason #1:
Uncle Harry's Hard-Line Approach
Will Be, Must Be, Inconsistent

The first problem with Uncle Harry's use of punishment is that even Uncle Harry cannot, *and should not*, be consistent with it. Straight punishment would be too inhuman without the inconsistencies of warnings and threats.

If Uncle Harry's swats were as consistent and quick as, say, an electric shock, he might make some short-term progress. Misused wall outlets and lamp sockets consistently punish you without warning; they don't hesitate because you look cute trying to be "devilish." They don't think you've had a bad day or haven't been reminded lately of what will happen if you touch them. We get none of this consideration, and we all stay away from them.

> *Out of love and sympathy, neither Mom, Dad, nor Uncle Harry can resist preceding punishments with warnings and threats.*

But Uncle Harry is not a wall socket. Out of love and sympathy, neither Mom, Dad, nor Uncle Harry can resist preceding punishments with the warnings and threats that become part of the game.

Parental consistency is always desirable and basic to learning. The lack of consistent reactions, on the reward side, leads to confusion and slows the pace of progress. The inevitable inconsistency on the punishment side brings on additional problems.

Remember that "mean" teacher you had in school? He, or

maybe it was a "she," used punishments, reprimands, sarcastic remarks, put-downs, and embarrassments whenever the kids deviated from the desirable, and sometimes even when kids had done nothing wrong. I bet you hated that class!

A student's greatest fear is to be embarrassed in front of the class. With "Mr. Meany," you just couldn't be sure when you might trigger an embarrassing reaction. *All* behaviors (even volunteering right answers, suggestions, or questions) were reduced because you and your friends wouldn't risk it. Not surprisingly, most "mean" teachers think the children in their classes are not very smart.

> *Parents in this pitfall soon find that "looking mad" won't do, and they have to act "really mad."*

When punishment is uncertain, children become cautious, especially when they are around the person who punishes. But around other people, a child's bad behavior may increase to let off the oppressed steam or to somehow even the score.

Parents also can fall into the "mean teacher" pattern, and their children may learn to behave whenever Mom threatens or looks mad. As Mom realizes this works, she may take up "looking (and acting) mad" most of the time. Parents in this pitfall soon find that "looking mad" won't do, and they have to act "really mad." **Now Mom has been pushed up a notch toward becoming a behavior problem herself!**

So for Nancy and Martin to grow into happy, independent, productive adults, they need opportunities to do more interesting activities than their "Let's-see-what-we-can-get-away-with" game. Mom and Dad need to catch opportunities to encourage their kids, limiting the use of punishment with alternatives such as allowing them to make amends for mistakes as we adults do. More on alternatives in Chapter 9.

Carrying out all of this is much more difficult and requires a lot more planning than hard-headed Uncle Harry's idea of "thrashing it out of them."

Reason #2:
The Trigger for Punishment Is Often Parent Feelings, not the Child's Behavior

In most parenting situations, punishment is likely to be more related to the frustrations and moods of the parent than to the mistakes of the child. Frequent use of punishment, when Dad or Mom have had it *up to here*, usually results in children who are more interested in the moment-to-moment mood of their parents than they are in their own rights and wrongs. They will watch, drive their parents down the road to misery, and come up just short of the boiling points of Mom and Dad.

Children then become manipulators who know that as long as they don't push too far, they're safe. They find that they can better predict punishment by watching their parents' emotions than by respecting agreements and requests. The parent-child relationship suffers because the practice of "punish-when-I've-had-it" tempts children to react to parents with disrespect, silence, and deceit, and to avoid them altogether whenever possible.

This does not make for a very pleasant family atmosphere.

> *Punishment is likely to be more related to the frustrations and moods of the parent than to the mistakes of the child.*

Reason #3:
Children Imitate

We usually think of a child's imitation of parents as very specific. *"Look at the way he walks, just like his dad." "Look at the way she does her hair, trying to be just like Mom!"*

But copying Mom and Dad is more likely to involve social habits. How does Mom handle situations when things don't go right? What is her solution when others don't do what she wants? If Dad gets frustrated, how does he react?

We all know how quickly kids will pick up those words of frustration when Dad hits himself on the kitchen drawer, but they also pick up the cues on *how to react* when

> *Teaching how to react to others by imitation may be more important than correcting the mistake itself!*

things go wrong. Kids can get the message that punishment (used by Mom and Dad) is a good way to deal with people.

The imitation of punishment will include the child's social life. How should a child handle friends when they don't do the "right thing?" *"It works for Mom; maybe it will work for me."* In any case, the most natural reflex to punishment is to give some back. If it is not possible to punish the parent, the child will turn to others.

So there's the possibility that our child will pick up cues from our behavior about what the appropriate reaction to unwanted behavior is. If a daughter frequently criticizes and yells at her baby brother, a careful observation of the parents' own reactions might be a clue as to where the daughter's reactions come from. When we slip now and then and react in anger, the risk is that this behavior may be imitated.

Children make a lot of mistakes: being led into errors by peers, forgetting chores and commitments, indulging in unhealthy foods, and wasting time, to mention a few. **When parents see so many errors, it's difficult to be accepting and look to the long run. But sometimes the goal of teaching how to react to others by imitation may be more important than correcting the mistake itself.**

Reason #4:
Punishment is Insulting, Belittling, and Lowers a Child's Value of Himself

The emotional put-down of punishment distracts the child from learning about the desired behavior. The punishment act is itself childish and belittles the significance and power of the person who is punished. **That's why *adults* are so insulted if you try punishment on them!**

Many parents have seen this downturn in a child's value of himself as he progresses through school. If a teacher's criticism is too severe, the child's value of himself starts to go down, the fear starts up, and a new disadvantage for learning develops.

The fear of failure begins to reduce the childhood process of trial and error. Discoveries in school subjects and in learning to get along with others come from a lot of guesses. How much guessing will a frightened child do? Once a child is discouraged and engaged in self-degrading thoughts, parents and teachers know learning will be slow.

Here's an example from the animal world of this broader negative effect of punishment. For many years I taught a college course in animal learning. Students had to teach their own pigeon to perform tasks by rewarding small successes. The exercise used seeds as a reward to get the pigeon to peck a plastic disc. At first the students gave the pigeon seeds for stepping toward the disc, then putting its head toward it, then touching it, and finally pecking the disc.

Sometimes students had trouble with the project because their pigeon was too scared to even move in its cage. If it had been handled roughly or temporarily escaped and had to be chased down before being put in the learning cage, it was too upset to do anything. *Pigeons that won't do anything can't be taught anything!* The student stared at the pigeon waiting for a chance to reward success. The pigeon stared at the student waiting for a chance to get out! The solution was usually a new effort in careful handling and generous rewards for even the smallest movements to explore the cage, followed by rewards for exploring the plastic disc, etc.

> *Once a child is discouraged and engaged in self-degrading thoughts, parents and teachers know learning will be slow.*

Punishment can produce the same impasse between a child and a parent. And the solution, in principle, is similar as well: careful handling and generous support.

Reason #5:
Punishment Encourages Stress Behaviors

Punishment will encourage bad habits such as nail-biting, hair-twirling, and "safer obsessions" with video games and TV. These "escapes" are very stubborn habits maintained by their usefulness for avoiding contact with the punisher. Whenever encouragement and reward are low, these stress behaviors will increase. Stress behaviors can attract some parental attention, and we are on our way to a new long-term problem.

Reason #6:
The Power Struggle

Punishment will tempt the child to react to the parent with disrespect; dealing with the disrespect then takes over the family airways leaving little time for positive interactions and learning. The parent can "win" the power struggle, but **for every winner a loser is made!**

The power struggle of punishment can spread to all family members. As others pick up the habit, a competition develops: Who can "outdo" (put down, criticize, reprimand, catch more mistakes of) whom? It ruins the family as a nurturing place where learning is encouraged through practice—*with* mistakes.

Reason #7:
It's a Short-term Trap That Can Last Forever

The parental bad habit of using punishment can be stubborn because it produces short-term results. For example, Martin has aggravated his Aunt Hazel all day and now refuses to get in the car to go home. Harried Hazel grabs Martin, gives him a little extra squeeze, and roughly deposits him in his seat. For the moment, we have progress—Martin is closer to home! Martin's bad behavior is temporarily stopped, Hazel has released a little tension, and maybe Hazel has "taught Martin a lesson" or at least evened the score.

The long-term disadvantages of Hazel's punishment habit will grow slowly. Martin will start the bad escape habits, he will feel worse about himself and about Aunt Hazel, and he will try to use punishment himself to "get even." These two people are well on the way to a poor relationship where Martin dodges some of Aunt Hazel's punishment by watching for her boiling point. Aunt Hazel boils over now and then to gain temporary relief from

Martin's bad moments. Martin will learn when to let up a little, and, when he's big enough, he will learn to imitate her punishment to gain more control.

Reason #8:
Discrimination

A child subjected to a parent in the "looking angry, acting angry" escalation learns the signals well. Innocent baby sitters and also teachers become fair game until they learn how to scowl miserably enough to get control. An additional social problem is now added because parents and others don't like to be forced to act mad and would rather not be around the child because they don't like the person they must become to keep control.

> *A negative, critical and threatening boss will have a reputation as a hardliner but who wants to please her?*

As you will see in the next section, **the parent suffers most from the frequent punishment policy, and the child may suffer less because he learns to adjust to people who will play his game and those who will not.**

We all develop discriminations and act differently with different people. But when punishment is used, we do our best to avoid the punishing person altogether. **A negative, critical and threatening boss will have a reputation as a hardliner but the employees will duck and dodge her as much as possible and give no extra effort.** Who wants to please her?

The relationship that develops is one in which two people only barely tolerate each other because they are forced to. A child would like to escape such a situation because of the possibility of being punished, and the parent would rather be away (at work, at meetings, or just out anywhere) because of the uncomfortable parental reactions that seem to be demanded by the situation.

Reason #9:
Relatives Will Go Home,
Parents Will Be Left Behind

When "Get Tough" Uncle Harry finally leaves, Mom and Dad are left with the long-term side effect of punishments that have been too frequent and severe for the child to cope with. The child's solution may be to stop responding altogether or, at least, to respond as little as possible.

> *With punishment you have to find your child; when you use praise, your child finds you.*

The situation has produced a kind of success, the child *is* quiet. He is a very quiet child whose few tentative responses are likely to be pounced on with reprimands and corrections.

Even if the adults try a better approach later on, the child may now refuse to risk coming out of his shell. The biggest wish of this child is to get out—out of the room, out of sight, or out of the house, if possible. Wouldn't we all rather dodge the punishment?

With punishment you have to find your child; when you use positive responses, your child finds you. Through repeated experience, the situation preceding punishment signals a child to start withdrawing. It could be a classroom, a house, a time of day, a particularly dangerous person, or a combination of these. Once experiences have taught the child these signals, the mere termination of punishment is not likely to be effective immediately because the child will be unwilling to take risks to find out if danger has passed. Now the fear may seem unreasonable, but the only solution the child is willing to accept is withdrawal, a chance to get out of the situation entirely.

Uncle Harry and Aunt Hazel will also leave behind other unintended effects. Activities and behaviors that explore new opportunities for learning may also be reduced because they now seem dangerous.

Often only your opinion of your son or daughter is understood in punishment. The details of *why* you are so angry are smothered in your child's emotion, fear, and desire to suppress the memory of the whole experience. Combine the lack of understanding with the fear of risking punishment, and we are well on the way to losing all learning opportunities.

Left on their own with Harry's punishment advice, parents will be tempted to increase the punishment when the children don't seem to get the message. Many small children just can't seem to get on the right wavelength to figure out when Dad or Mom is mad, acting mad, or *really* mad. Consistencies may be there, but the child just doesn't see them.

Punishment provides very little information. It only tells you one of the things you ought *not* to do, nothing about what *to do*. With so little to go on, the child could decide to ignore and forget these painful moments as soon as possible. We've all known a little Nancy or Martin whose mother increases reprimands, corrects, grabs, and sends him or her into confinement almost continually. Most of the time, if a child doesn't understand, he or she does whatever impulse comes to his or her little mind while Mom or Dad escalate the punishment.

Reason #10:
It Leads to the Ultimate Punishment—
Divorce of Parent from Child

Victims of punishment want to escape. This may not always be obvious because they may have reasons for not just scratching at the nearest door. But any child being punished has one thought in mind, *"Get away!"*

No matter what effect punishment may have in the short run, the parents must look ahead to losing their child. That's why these strategies usually don't work on adults—adults can leave. But if the leaving option is not possible, then our victim may move on to other ways of escape. A child could withdraw to his room or to a special place, and even a teen could withdraw to a corner of his mind to daydream.

Parents can anticipate what's on the mind of a child threatened with punishment and will usually decorate the punishment with,

> *No matter what effect punishment may have in the short run, the parents must look ahead to losing their child.*

"As long as you live in this house..." or *"You're not so big that I can't..."* The implication is that the parent is counting on some other aspect of the situation to keep the child within range for punishment. Either the doors must be locked, literally or figuratively, or the parents' rewards are enough to compensate for the unhappiness.

But the separation seems to be a risk the parent is willing to take, and the separation is one the child is temporarily looking for. The conflict and confusion are intensified because your home is their most important source of security.

So don't appear to be considering divorce from your children.

This ultimate consequence is too disturbing and implies that your value of your child can be easily traded away. Your love and loyalty have a higher price tag and should not become part of bluffing or bargaining.

So Why Would Anyone Use Punishment?

With all these discouraging problems, you might wonder why some parents continue to use punishment. Even parent behavior should diminish when it is unsuccessful. So when their action (punishment) doesn't work, why don't they just quit?

The answer is that in the very short term, punishment produces some results. If Mom punishes Fred for throwing sand while playing in the sandbox, Mom's punishment is reinforced by its immediate effect of interrupting Fred's bad behavior temporarily.

Fred, a little more afraid and confused, may start biting his nails. His stress habit will attract some attention, and we are creating an unpleasant routine supported by subtle short-term benefits. For Mom there is the brief respite and for Fred there is parental attention for his nail-biting, and he has the added benefit of less blame, responsibility or guilt because he "paid the price."

How to Reverse Uncle Harry's Effects

When the situation has been dangerous for a long time, a reduction in punishment must be accompanied with an increase in opportunities for genuine encouragement. For the child made this timid, very minor events can act as punishments. Simply interrupting him when he intends to say something at dinner may silence him for the whole meal. A verbal snap from his sibling may accomplish the same thing.

It will require many isolated one-on-one moments with generous parents showing great tolerance and support to draw him out. The isolated sessions can affect other family situations. For example, the parent might begin with a daily habit of games and puzzles and book reading in a special place alone with the child. Once the one-on-one sessions have been successful, the parents could try letting others back into the situation.

9
Five Alternatives to Punishment

> If you come to my house for dinner tonight
> and spill your drink at the table, you don't
> expect me to say: *"Hey! What do you think
> you're doing? You're so clumsy! Now pay
> attention to what you're doing or I'll send
> you home!"*

What nerve! Treating a guest like a child. What happened to
"the benefit of the doubt?" You expect to be allowed to make
amends; you expect me to belittle the problem; you even expect
sympathy: *"Oh, too bad. No problem, I'll get a cloth."* You say,
"I'm sorry, let me get that. I'll take care of it." **Isn't adulthood
nice?**

We all deal with unwanted adult behavior every day, but most
of us have given up punishment of the straightforward kind, long
ago. The culture we live in continues to provide some punishment—"logical consequences" we sometimes call them—and the
courts hand out punishments for the larger transgressions. But

logical consequences and court sentences are usually long delayed and given only for repeated bad habits and big mistakes.

So with unwanted *adult* behavior, what alternatives to punishment do we use? **Every day, adult mistakes receive *very kind* reactions.** Even blowing your horn in traffic is considered too aggressive. Often we just allow the person to make amends, or we ignore the mistake altogether. If we control the situation, we might try to make it less likely he will repeat the mistake: *"The boss should give better instructions. He should put up more signs if the printer needs service too often."* After more instruction, the boss may use warnings: *"Anyone caught putting their sandwich in the printer will be ...."* and then, maybe, punishment.

> *Since punishment has so many disadvantages anyway, let's get on to a more adult way of handling problems.*

Along with *making amends*, we'll also take up the pros and cons of *ignoring,* adding a *guarantee for good behavior*, *changing the convenience,* and using *"count-outs and time-outs."* **Since punishment has so many disadvantages anyway, let's get on to a more adult way of handling problems.**

Alternative #1:
Making Amends

Making amends is the number one strategy adults use to handle bad adult behavior. **When adults make a blunder, we would rather have the offender try again than punish him.** At what age did you earn such consideration? Reactions to mistakes, by kids, teens, or adults, accidental or not, should start with allowing the blunderer to make amends. A child deserves the same respect. It is only fair to assume he is doing his best.

Grandma: (Sitting down to dinner) *"Whoops. <u>Now</u> I know what I forgot at the store—coffee! But we have juice, how about that?"*

Mom: *"Don't worry about it, juice is fine. We'll get the coffee tomorrow."* (Mom minimizes mistake)

Grandma: *"At least I'll get out the juice."* (Grandma makes amends)

Nancy: *"Hey! Mobby licked my spoon when I had it down there."*

Grandma: *"Don't use it now that the dog licked it! Keep your hands up to the table! You're going back in your high chair if you don't have enough sense to ..."*

Mom: (Interrupting) *"Nancy, just get down and get yourself another spoon."* (And then to Grandma) *"I can get along without the coffee until tomorrow if you can. So no problem, right?"*

Grandma: *"What? Oh, ah, yes, OK, OK. If I get a break on forgetting the coffee, I guess Nancy gets a break, too. And, Nancy, could you put the dog out while you're over there?"*

Alternative #2:
Ignoring

Ignoring bad behavior eventually decreases it, especially if the child was acting up to get attention. If a parent can tough it out and hold back attention for the bad behavior, the child will go on to something else. The problem here is that in the short run, *more bad behavior* is likely rather than less. This bad behavior has been a part of a habit to get entertainment or attention from Mom and

Dad. Now the parents plan to cut that off.

If the usual amount of acting up will no longer work, the child may escalate the volume. At the higher intensity, the parents may break the new rule and punish this outrageous behavior.

If that quiets things down, the parents may return to the ignoring rule only to go back to punishment when the volume again reaches their pain threshold. The process builds up a new level of bad behavior. **Escalation is a very common problem because the natural childish reaction to failure (to get attention) is to try harder.**

If you use a vending machine at work and one day it doesn't work, what do you do? Calmly give up? Or jab and yank on the coin return and bang on the little buttons. After your mini-tantrum, you look around for another solution to the problem—another machine or another store. You know plenty of sources for what you want so you quit acting "like a kid" and go on to another solution.

What's available for your child when he finds his bad behavior no longer works?

Now what's available for your child when he finds his bad behavior no longer works his personal "vending machines?" Your child thinks, *"If the usual volume isn't working, maybe I should add some really loud screams!"* He's going to escalate, then look for another solution. What will he find? **What can be added to ignoring so it will work?**

Alternative #3:
Ignoring Some of the Bad, Guaranteeing Some of the Good

As a tantrum subsides, a child finally begins to cast about for a new solution. What he finds and latches on to will depend on the parents' understanding of the outcome their child is looking for.

If the child is in need of attention, the situation will not be made better if our strategy, overall, reduces attention. We should make a mental note to respond to new behaviors whenever we plan to ignore unwanted behavior.

> *A child isn't much closer to the correct behavior by being ignored or told, "Wrong!"*

Mom and Dad need a plan to encourage good behaviors and should be alert to the first opportunity to work the plan. Ignoring the unwanted behavior *and* planning to encourage *specific, likely,* successes will produce a better result. The message needs to be clear: *"Now that's a good way to handle that!" "I liked hearing about your report on the Civil War battle. You're learning about interesting things." "I noticed you helped clear the table after supper. That's great!"*

Positive reactions give your child a clear message about what to do. Punishment gives less information. Considering all the possibilities for error, **a child isn't much closer to the correct behavior by just being ignored or told, *"Wrong!"***

Chapter 3 covered some advantages of watching for successful behavior and providing good positive feedback when it occurs. That "catch 'em being good" notion can be particularly useful when you apply the ignoring strategy for an unwanted behavior.

Practice and experience are the core of child development, but they only continue with positive consequences for each success. It can be tiresome and frustrating to a parent to let a child practice a task, foul it up, and do it again. **Making a seven-year-old's bed is so much easier than coaxing him to try it and make a mess of it. Telling a ten-year-old girl what to wear is easier than sending her back for another look to replace inappropriate clothing probably with other inappropriate clothing.**

The situation can be particularly difficult when enthusiastic encouragement and reward must be provided for the first poor approximations of the ideal behavior, but the need for these reactions is crucial—this kind of practice is absolutely imperative. It would be nice if, after a little practice, children would continue to perform on their own, but we must provide continuous encouragement in order to enjoy continuous improvement. **You must always be a rewarding parent just as you must always be a rewarding spouse or friend.**

Children try new behaviors every day to find the adjustment that seems right. Perhaps as a child you remember thinking, *"When I make mistakes everyone notices and I get in trouble, but a lot of times I do well, and nobody ever says a thing."* To prevent unwanted behaviors, parents need to "catch 'em being good," not just when the desired behavior occurs, but when a behavior in the right direction comes along.

Actions that are improvements and steps forward need the most encouragement, recognition, praise, and reward. Be realistic about where to start the encouragement. In the "catch 'em being good" alternative, you need to start rewarding at the child's level now, and then move toward the improvements. A kid who stays in her room most of the time will not change if criticized, but may come out more often if she finds appreciation and activities she likes when she is in the family areas of the house. **Few people can resist sincere praise.**

Alternative #4:
Using the Cost of Inconvenience

Many little inconveniences, particularly those for older children and adults, may seem at first trivial, but when put into practice, they can be extremely effective. For example, if Dad has to put a penny in a jar on the kitchen table every time he loses his temper, it may seem trivial for someone with plenty of pennies. But if the rule is strictly followed, the inconvenience of having to stop, get a penny, and go into the kitchen and put it in the jar can be a very effective consequence. **It's not the money but the behavioral "cost" that makes this consequence work.**

As a strategy for removing or reducing smoking behavior in adults, many psychologists use the principle of inconvenience. The heavy smoker is instructed to keep an exact record of his smoking throughout each day. He carries a little notebook wherever he goes and writes down the time, to the minute, when he takes out a cigarette, and the time he puts it out. He may be asked to note the situation as well, including who was with him and what he was doing. Some psychologists also ask for the cigarette butts to be saved and brought in for counting. These tasks may not seem like consequences as we have talked about them so far, but they are consequences of a most useful type—they require time. **A smoker may be too busy to make all those entries and save butts, so he takes a pass on having that cigarette.**

> *It's not the money but the behavioral "cost" that makes this consequence work.*

Such a self-administered procedure requires a very cooperative and trustworthy subject. I found the "cost-of-inconvenience" procedure more useful with smokers referred to me who have been told by their doctor that their health or even their life is at stake.

They usually *want* the process to work and they can be counted on to try hard. The procedure has not worked well when used on people who "feel they should cut down" or quit for the children's sake. With these less motivated people, it takes a stronger procedure than "the cost of inconvenience."

Children can be less motivated to change, but sometimes they can be enthusiastic about record-keeping which can be a version of the cost of inconvenience procedure. One mother reported that her 19-year-old son, Damon, continually disrupted the family by "checking things." On some evenings, he insisted on checking as many as 70 things before going to sleep. Damon checked to see if the back door was locked. He checked to see if the light was out in the basement. He checked to see if his pen was on his desk and if his dresser drawers were closed. Some of this would have been reasonable, but the situation got out of hand when he checked the same thing for the fifth or sixth time in the same evening!

> *Because of the work and inconvenience of the procedure, the number of times Damon checked things soon was down to a level that was only a little unusual.*

Some progress was made by reducing Damon's parents' attention to the excessive checking and increasing conversation time before he went to bed. The most effective procedure was beginning a record of every item checked, the time it was checked, the result of the check, and what could have happened if the item had been left unchecked.

The procedure involved so much writing and decision-making that it was nearly impossible to check 70 things each evening. Because of the work and inconvenience of the procedure, Damon began to pass up the items that were not so important and he made a special effort to remember the ones already checked or to look at his record, so that he didn't have to do it again. The number of times Damon checked things soon was down to a level that was only a little unusual instead of disruptive to the family.

The same principle of inconvenience can be used to increase a habit. For example, good homework habits can be influenced by how convenient it is to get started. If there is a place to do homework with little distraction and paper to work with, then we have a better chance of getting some homework done.

> Dianne: *"I'm not going to practice this stupid violin any more, it's too much trouble!"*
>
> Mom: *"Just another ten minutes, then you can quit."*
>
> Dianne: *"Phooey."*

Dianne's practice is best done in intervals that keep frustration to a minimum, but once Dianne begins, Mom hates to let her quit because it's such a hassle to get her to start again. **Maybe Mom could do away with some inconveniences associated with Dianne's practice.** She could help Dianne get out the music and set up the stand. Then while Dianne checks the tuning, Mom could turn off the TV and get everyone else out of the room. If some of these inconveniences to starting could be done away with, maybe Dianne would practice more frequently.

> Mom: *"Let's set up a special place for you. How about in our bedroom? We're never in there when you need to practice and it's away from the TV and your brother. You can leave your music stand out, and it won't be disturbed."*
>
> Dianne: *"OK, but I still think all this practice is stupid."*

We have not solved the violin problem by just finding a place to practice. Dianne is going to need more encouragement than that. Mom needs to visit the practice situation a lot, comment on the progress, and help the instructor make practice of interest to Dianne. But **a place to practice easily, and without frustrating start-up time, is a step toward making it all happen.**

Alternative #5: Count-outs and Time-outs

Sometimes the bad behavior demands a reaction. We don't let adults get away with just anything and children shouldn't be misled that anything goes either. What alternative is there when the mistakes should not be ignored, and making amends or hoping for opportunities for encouragement is not enough?

For young children time-out is often a good solution. We all know the drill of putting the child on a chair or in his/her room for a little "cooling off" and isolation as a kind of punishment. The procedure can work well if the threats, arguments, and other verbal decorations that often precede the time-out can be kept to a minimum.

Mom:	(Liz throws a toy at her sister.) *"Liz! We don't throw toys. You could hurt someone. That's One!"* (Liz throws again.) *"Liz, I told you, that's <u>Two</u>."*
Liz:	*"I don't <u>want</u> it!"* (Liz throws again.)
Mom:	*"OK, that's Three."* Mom takes Liz to the kitchen chair and deposits her there.

Mom is doing well. She doesn't talk much during the count which could lead Lisa to act up more; she doesn't make a lot of threats, and she corrects Liz in a way that can be used frequently— no dramatic punishment that requires a big build-up.

How long should Liz remain in the chair? A very short time would be best. **Many parents have found the act of starting the time-out, putting the child in the chair or room, is the effective part.** Prolonged isolation is probably not effective because the child forgets exactly what it was all about. The situation will have changed so much after a long isolation that there will be no opportunity to practice anything right. *Ten or 15 seconds* is enough for two-year-olds, and one minute is enough for four, five, and six-year-olds. The message was sent when the prompt decision was made at the count of three (or ten, if that's the rule).

> *Many parents have found the act of starting the time-out is the effective part.*

The same counting can be used for an ongoing behavior: Duncan starts rocking on top of a wobbly chair and Mom says, *"Duncan, that's dangerous, stop it."* If Duncan doesn't stop, Mom says, *"Duncan, stop. That's dangerous. OK, that's one... two...three...four..."* If Duncan is still at it at ten, Duncan goes to time-out.

All of these strategies require effort, and some are downright hard work so make sure you eliminate any trivial behaviors from your rule before you start a plan.

When Tim insisted on always using a fork to eat, even when it was chunky soup, his parents didn't like it but felt he had the choice. In their weekly planning session they agreed the use of a fork was unimportant and decided to make nothing of it. The "problem" was too trivial, and they decided *any* rule or reaction was too much. But when he hit his younger sister, they reacted strongly and used the time-out method.

Their different reactions to these very different behaviors keep the family atmosphere from becoming cluttered with unnecessary criticism of trivial temporary problems. Yet it's obvious that Mom and Dad care and will not tolerate bad behavior.

A Count-Down for Martin. Martin always shows off and acts silly when company comes or the family goes visiting. He makes a fool of himself while watching his parents for their boiling point. He knows he can go further than usual and he knows Mom and Dad's boiling point **is a much better predictor of real punishment than his own foolishness.** Martin has gained some control over the situation. True, it's miserable for everyone, but he likes being the focus *and* in control.

Two factors keep Martin's parents from getting the upper hand. One, the punishments they might have in mind are too severe for frequent use: sending him off to his room for a long time (too rejecting), leaving him in the car when visiting (too dangerous), or swatting him (too hard on the social situation). So most of the time they use threats which only tell Martin how far he has to go.

The second factor is that *Mom and Dad need specific definitions of what is right* so they can encourage Martin. *They also need a definition of what is wrong* so that if any reaction is to be used, it comes because of what Martin does, not for what his behavior *does to* his parents. Pinning down these definitions will put consistency back in the situation and return control to Mom and Dad.

The less severe "count-out-time-out" method is easier to use with specific definitions of expected behavior. For example, when the family goes on visits, Mom could use the car as a time-out for Martin if she stays with him. If Mom reacts to Martin's improvements as well, we may be on our way to a better experience:

> Mom: *"Martin, if you act silly over at Aunt Hazel's, we're going to take a time-out in the car."*

Martin:	*"I'll be good."*
Dad:	*"We're here. Martin, why don't you carry your cousin Betty's present in?"*
Martin:	(At the door) *"Happy Terrible Birthday, Betty!"*
Mom:	*"Martin, that's one."*
Martin:	*"Well, it is terrible."*
Mom:	*"That's two and three. We're going back to the car, now!"*
Martin:	*"No, no, I'll be better. I'll play nice with Betty."*
Mom:	*"Sorry, the count's already done."*
Mom:	(After only one minute in the car) *"OK, let's go back in and see what we're missing. When it's dinner time, I'll call you and you can help me serve the salad we brought."*
Martin:	*"I'm going to <u>get</u> Betty."*
Mom:	*"Martin, the rule is still the same: three counts and I'll have to take you to the car again—no extra chances."*

Will Martin be an angel the rest of the day? Probably not, but Mom and Dad have a plan, and Martin is not going to be allowed to take over and continually ruin their visit. After a few visits, Mom and Dad's combination of time-outs and encouragements will win out or Martin may be left home with a babysitter.

Bedtime as a Time-Out Or Not?

Bedtime is not a moment when you need the extra disadvantage of a child's bad attitude resulting from being sent to bed as punishment. How can being sent to bed be used as a punishment at one time and sold as something the child should *want* at another? Putting a child to bed should not be used as a time-out.

The Work of Being a Parent

Allowing a child to make amends, using count-outs, or ignoring and looking for something good *all* require diligent effort. Contrary to the easy magical advice from aunts, uncles, and some professionals, being a parent can be downright hard work. So make sure you eliminate rules concerning trivial behaviors before you start any of these plans.

Aunt Hazel and Uncle Harry won't be easily satisfied with these alternatives in this chapter. But they would also be disappointed in the results of punishment. Neither punishment nor these alternatives will produce the instant change they want.

The best parental strategy will include:
- **supporting the desirable,**
- **ignoring the tolerable, and**
- **reacting with consistency to the intolerable.**

This plan will give the children a good model to follow as well as a way to learn. They will become more competent and pleasant people.

Exercise and Summary for T-3
TAKE ON Just a Few Good Rules

A Planning Session Agenda

Planning sessions have a dangerous tendency to turn into general gripe sessions. Although complaining can be therapeutic, parents often jump around from one problem to another without concluding a plan for any particular one.

So a planning session needs an agenda that will focus on planning parental reactions to a particular situation. The session should also produce an overall understanding of what is going on when the specific problem is encountered.

This exercise will help you do a complete "walk-through" of a problem you identified in the earlier exercises. You may not always need such a complete analysis, but to be alert to the possible aspects of behavior, this exercise will include all the steps.

A. First select a behavior from your priority list in Exercise T-2 (page 81), **then fill out a Behavior Chart as you did in Exercise T-1** (page 28).

You will not yet have a record of the behavior as described in the last part of the chart, but you can put down your own observations as you remember them to answer thequestions:

1. What is an objective description of the behavior?
2. What triggers the problem?
3. What happens next?
4. Where would you place the possible blame or credit?
5. At what age would you expect an average child to do what you are hoping will be done in this situation?
6. How could you allow more practice?
7. When do problems happen? (keep record)

B. Review the following check list for consequences as you consider possible reactions to the behavior. Pose each question on the planning session agenda:

1. **Is the problem big enough to bother with?**
   Remember, a "No" here should indicate a strategy—a strategy to eliminate nagging your child or yourself about the problem.

2. **Am I attempting too much at one time?**
   A tempting pitfall in parenting is to try to make too many changes at the same time. Don't attempt to control eating, piano practicing, bed-making, and doing homework all at once. Concentrating on too many plans leads to mistakes and too much "policing." Think small. Begin with one rule at a time.

3. **Can I influence the behavior in an easier way?**
   Some worrisome behaviors can be reduced simply by engineering the environment. For example, you could set aside a special kitchen drawer of safe utensils for a son or daughter's cooking projects. This may be easier than worrying about the child's finding and handling dangerous or fragile tools.

4. **Have I thought of all the consequences that could be maintaining the behavior?**
   What usually happens when the "bad" behavior occurs and what happens next? What usually happens if she performs correctly? If you select a new consequence, how should you set up the practice?

5. Is it a one-shot consequence?

A one-shot consequence is a promise of something good or threat of something bad in the distant *future*. Whether a threat or promise, it has the same disagreeable characteristics: it is not repeatable, it tempts the parents to use repeated threats and it will probably be somewhat arbitrary in the end. And then the next day what should you do? Start a new threat?

6. Is the consequence too severe?

You want something that can be used easily and repeatedly. So don't make plans when you're still angry over a mistake. Paying attention to only bad behavior won't help. Plan to reward good behaviors reasonably and react to bad ones reasonably.

7. If ignoring is the plan, are you prepared to handle your child's reaction?

If tantrums are to be ignored, what will you pay attention to?

8. Is your expectation reasonable?

Are you starting with a behavior simple enough to ensure that rewards can occur—even on the first day? Even if it is reasonable, it may still be much more than your daughter has ordinarily been doing. She was used to nibbling so don't make the sudden unreasonable demand of filling her plate and telling her no dessert until she finishes. Remember to start where *she* is, not where you *wish* her to be.

9. Is the consequence too weak?

What can be done if your child just doesn't seem to care

about the new consequence? It could be that you are not sticking to the rule and he really doesn't *have* to care. Or possibly he has too many freebies available (*"If I can't go out, I'll watch TV!"*).

C. Review this Check List for Alternatives to Punishment.

1. Could you use the adult reaction to mistakes, *making amends*?
2. Is it possible to first try *ignoring*?
3. Before going on to harder work, could you model the good behavior for your child?
4. Have the other possibilities presented in the preceding chapter been considered: *"Catch 'em being good,"* *"changing the convenience"* of the behavior, and using *"count-outs and time-outs."*

T-4
TEACH WELL
with Good Listening
and Good Coaching

Social habits and skills don't come naturally. Children will learn how to get along in the world through the advice and example of their parents. This training is too important to leave to chance, so parents will need a lot of information about what is going on with their children. Through careful listening and communication, parents can find opportunities to coach, teach and pass along good advice.

10
Listening Before Teaching:
A Requirement for Successful Parenting

If it is language that makes us human,
one-half of language is to listen.

—Jacob Trapp

The Crucial Growing Up Question:
"Mom (Dad), Can We Talk?"

If we meet someday and you tell me you used only one idea from this book, I hope it is from this section about listening skills. With open, available lines of communication, most of the fairness, influence, and negotiation described in the other chapters can be worked out.

Vulnerable. That is a feeling familiar to all children. They know they have much to learn, and they know they are making many mistakes because they are encountering so much at one time. **Who is a safe confidant? Who can a son or daughter go to with problems? Who will be tolerant and uncritical like a friend,**

and yet be helpful with suggestions from experience like an adult?

Most parents meet the requirement of experience, but to be heard, a parent also needs to be tolerant and uncritical. That's why the first requirement of tolerance and acceptance is needed in the earliest years and in the earliest part of each conversation.

> *Who will be tolerant and uncritical like a friend and yet be helpful with suggestions from experience like an adult?*

The beginning of a talk about a problem is the most risky moment for a child because of his vulnerability and possible embarrassment. What should your first reaction be? If I were your child, I would hope that you would "hear me out" in presenting the story or problem, that you would not become critical or try to place the blame quickly.

Some of the listening skills presented below may already be familiar to you, but it is important to quality parenting to have a list of them handy. Also, new tips for keeping an open communication with your child are given special attention here.

Stop, Look, and Listen

What can parents *do* to signal their child that they are listening? Before discussing what you *say* that sends the *"I hear you"* message, let's look at two important things you should *do* before saying anything.

Eye Contact. It's nerve-wracking to have a person stare at you while you're talking, but a person who always looks somewhere else also frustrates their conversational partner. For good eye contact, put aside the newspaper, turn off the TV, and face the person to show you are listening. This will keep your mind on the topic and on the other skills given below.

Always face up to your listening responsibility! In order to look at some one, you have to face him or her. It can be casual; there's no need to be "in their face" through the whole talk, but we all know the uncomfortable feeling when someone becomes distracted or actually walks away while we struggle to keep up and finish what we want to say.

Along with facing your child, be aware of other aspects of posture that send the wrong messages. Slumping, stretching, and fidgeting all indicate a lack of attention. Once you've established good habits of eye contact and facing your child, focus on your conversational style.

> *Your style of conversation sends a message about how you feel about your partner in conversation.*

First of all, your style of conversation sends a message about how you feel about your partner in conversation. Children are forever on guard to protect their fragile self-confidence. They're on the lookout for your evaluation of them as a person first; the subject of the conversation, that we think is the whole point, takes second place. The child may be totally preoccupied with extracting your *personal* evaluation for the first few sentences. If the signals are negative, up come the defensive reactions before any useful exchange begins.

Mom:	*"So did you play nice with Kevin at his house?"*
Walt:	*"Yes."*
Mom:	*"You didn't fight with him?"*
Walt:	*"No, I <u>didn't</u>!"*
Mom:	*"Did you share?"*
Walt:	*"Yes, can I go now?"*

Mom's message here is that Walt may have been bad and she
wants to know so she can correct him. Walt has the message in the
first question and wants to leave. What happened over at Kevin's?
Did Kevin do something that Walt needs to learn how to handle?
Did anything unusual happen that Walt needs to have explained?
We may never know.

Second chance:

> Mom: *"Have a good time at Kevin's?"*
> Walt: *"Yeah."*
> Mom: *"What did you do?"*
> Walt: *"Just watched TV."*
> Mom: *"What? I didn't send you over there just to watch more TV!"*

Until TV gets into it, Mom was doing well. Let's give her
another chance on this last reaction. Walt didn't have complete
control over what he and Kevin did. **We don't know if watching
TV was Walt's fault, but the tone puts him on the defensive.**
Mom may not like the activity (if watching TV is an "activity"),
but bringing that into a conversation with Walt won't encourage
him to say much more. Instead Mom could say less:

Another chance:

> Mom: *"TV?"*
> Walt: *"Yeah, we got to fooling around and his sister fell off the couch."*
> Mom: *"Fell?"*
> Walt: *"Well, she was sort of pushed."*
> Mom: *"Everybody has to be careful around little ones, Walt. Kevin knows that because he has his sister there all the time."*

Here Mom separated *Walt* from Walt's *behavior*, making it easier on him, allowing him to learn something. Let's give Dad a chance:

> Donald: *"You should have seen what happened in gym today, Dad."*
>
> Dad: *"What, Donald?"*
>
> Donald: *"Keith got in an argument with Mr. Effort and they ended up in a real fight!"*
>
> Dad: *"I'm sure it wasn't much of a fight."*
>
> Donald: *"Yes it was! They were wrestling!"*
>
> Dad: *"I hope you didn't have anything to do with it."*
>
> Donald: *"Naw, all I did was cheer."*
>
> Dad: *"Cheer? Listen, Donald, you'll end up in trouble right along with Keith! Don't you have any more sense than to . . ."*

Let's interrupt Dad here just for a moment. **Donald, like all kids, resents the way his dad turned his story into a talk about the mistakes that Donald might have made.** The experience will reduce his talks with Dad in the future. Dad criticized his son's story: (1) he thought Donald was wrong because it wasn't much of a fight, (2) Donald probably had something to do with it, and (3) he shouldn't have cheered. Dad centered the conversation on what he disliked about his son's behavior instead of the story. All this happened in a 20-second discussion.

Our first rule of conversation is to avoid instant criticism. Let's back up and give Dad another chance to be more friendly, but still help Donald consider possible consequences of the gym-class experience.

Second chance:

> Donald: *"You should have seen what happened in gym today, Dad."*
>
> Dad: *"What happened, Donald?"*
>
> Donald: *"Keith got in an argument with Mr. Effort and they ended up in a real fight!"*
>
> Dad: *"How did it all start?"* (Dad ignores the possible exaggeration, doesn't express doubt, and shows interest instead.)
>
> Donald: *"They just started arguing about the exercises and Keith wouldn't give in."*
>
> Dad: *"Hard to win against the teacher."* (Dad comments in general, and suggests alternatives that are not critical of Donald.)
>
> Donald: *"Yeah, Keith is in big trouble."*
>
> Dad: *"Did they ever get around to the exercises?"* (Dad is interested in the story, not just in making points and giving advice.)
>
> Donald: *"Keith was sent to the office and then we tried these safety belts for the flips. Do you know about those?"*
>
> Dad: *"I don't think we had them in my school."*
>
> Donald: *"Well, you have these ropes..."*

Donald has a clearer view of the incident now and understands the hopelessness of Keith's argumentative attitude. **He wasn't distracted with defending himself when he told Dad the story.** And now he's explaining something to his father. Dad is showing respect for Donald and seems to think Donald has something interesting to say.

We all dislike instant evaluation, but young people are particularly self-centered and reactive to it. Some adults and almost all children fit into this category. The most important part of conversation for these people is: *"What does the message say about me."* **Young people "tune in" to parts of conversations—the parts about them, and they are less interested in the *content*.**

Many family conversations go wrong because the child reacts to the opinion expressed about him or her while *we* thought the *topics* were the important parts! So your children may learn that all conversations with you are safe because you seldom bring up their shortcomings and failures. Or they learn you always have a criticism or advice to give, and little talks with you should be avoided.

Use "It" Instead of "You"

People who use positive communication are "easy to talk to." They seem interested in the other person (they talk about, and ask about, the other person). If conversation becomes threatening, they make it comfortable by using the second rule of conversation: Try to look at a problem as an "it" instead of something about you or me. In other words, use neutral phrases such as, "it happened" or "what happened?" rather than, "What did *you* do?"

Mom:	*"How was art class today?"*
Morris:	*"Oh, OK, what I saw of it."*
Mom:	*"What do you mean?"*
Morris:	*"Mrs. Clay sent me to the office."*
Mom:	*"What did you do?"*
Morris:	*"I didn't do anything!"*
Mom:	*"You must have done something; you aren't sent to the office for nothing!"*
Morris:	*"You never think it could be the teacher's fault; you always blame me!"*

Mom:	*"What kind of talk is that? Let's have the whole story!"*
Morris:	*"Oh, nuts!"* (Morris stomps out.)

This conversation goes wrong when Mom asks personal and threatening questions such as, *"What do you mean?"* and *"What did you do?"* All of this would have come out eventually, but her impatience erased any chance for helping. Mom could do better by keeping the personal threat at a low level and talking about the problem as a an 'it' topic instead of a "you" topic:

Second chance:

Mom:	*"How was art class today?"*
Morris:	*"Oh, OK, what I saw of it."*
Mom:	*"You missed some of it?"*
Morris:	*"Mrs. Clay sent me to the office."*
Mom:	*"What happened?"* (Emphasizes the neutral word "What" instead of "you." *What* happened. This is much better than, "What did *YOU* do?")
Morris:	*"Tom ripped my paper."*
Mom:	*"Oh no!"* (Emphasizes sympathy rather than her child's upcoming mistake)
Morris:	*"Yeah, so I shoved him."*
Mom:	*"And so she sent you to the office?"* (Emphasizes the punishment without adding to it.)
Morris:	*"Yeah."*
Mom:	*"Then what happened?"*
Morris:	*"Well, for one thing, I'm behind in art again."*
Mom:	*"Well, if you can stay away from Tom maybe you'll catch up. What else happened today?"* (Adds a little parental advice and then on to looking for something more positive)

Use Reflective and Sympathetic Statements

Often a child's first remarks are only an expression of feelings and are short on facts. If a parent reacts with advice or opinion right away, the parent's response could be way off target. Reflective statements are useful in order to hear the child out.

The term, reflective, describes parental reactions that say nothing new, but simply repeat what the child said in different words. They send a message of *"I heard what you said."* They keep the conversation going and provide opportunities to get straightforward information without defensiveness. And the parent doesn't snatch control of the conversation away from the child. Let's look at an example of reflective statements in action by a mother learning about her daughter.

Brenda:	*"Man, is that school boring!"*
Mom:	*"It's really getting you down."* (Mom just uses different words for "boring"; this is reflective and tells her daughter she is listening.)
Brenda:	*"You bet."*
Mom:	*"What's getting you the most?"* (A good it-question starts with "what," instead of, "Why are YOU so bored?")
Brenda:	*"I don't know. I guess it's the whole thing."*
Mom:	*"You need a break."* (Good, sympathetic remark that avoids, "There must be something wrong (with you)!" That would be threatening.)
Brenda:	*"Yeah, but vacation is six weeks away."*
Mom:	*"That's a long time. Got any plans?"* (Good reflective statement that directs the conversation onto a positive topic.)
Brenda:	*"No."*

Mom: *"Hard to think that far ahead."* (A reflective
          statement that repeats "No plans" in different
          words; it is also sympathetic and friendly.)
Brenda: *"Pam is getting some applications for camps."*
Mom: *"Sounds like a good idea."*
Brenda: *"I might ask her about it."*

A complaint about boredom such as this is a familiar remark to
most parents. Although not much is solved about boredom in this
conversation, Mom has a better understanding of her daughter's
feelings and may be more tolerant. **She avoided the temptation
to "get something done" in this short talk.** Indirectly, Mom said
she has had similar feelings to her daughter's and it's all right to
have those. Most important, it's all right to talk to Mom about
feelings without being criticized for them."

**Because Mom has allowed her daughter to direct the topic,
information has flowed *to* her.** If *she* had directed the topic,
information would have flowed *from* her as advice, but she would
have learned very little about her daughter. Letting her daughter
direct the conversation now gives Mom the added benefit of a
"ticket of admission" to begin next time:

> *"Say, did Pam ever get any camp applications?"* or
> *"Only five weeks left now; how's it going?"*

**A few weeks and months of this effort from Mom and these
two will be good friends.** Notice there is no room for old complaints in this approach. The frequent complaints such as, *"You
shouldn't be bored!" "You never plan ahead like Pam!"* or out-of-
left-field old complaints such as: *"You never do your homework!"*
and *"You don't come when I call you"* should all be left out of
these conversations. Such criticisms are too broad, and therefore,

will be taken personally because they say, *"And while I'm thinking about you, another thing I don't like is…"* Instead Mom encouraged her daughter to take control of the conversation and parental complaints were postponed.

Caution: Arguments for Entertainment's Sake Can Be Habit-Forming!

In conversation and arguments, the answer as to whether a problem behavior is important enough to bother with is particularly important. Be sure to distinguish between what your child says and what he or she does. Intentions are *not* actions, but they can produce entertaining arguments.

Your child may want a reaction from you or just want to convince you that you can't do anything before you try. **Some of your child's behavior in school or other places is away from your influence and that could be one reason school and other outside activities are her favorite topics.**

Some of the more obnoxious stories may be re-designed for your ears alone, just to push your button or get you to argue! Most of the time your reaction should be mellow, especially regarding abstract or distant situations.

When Todd's father first talked to me, he told me Todd made rude remarks about his teachers which always resulted in a sharp reprimand from Dad. For example:

> Dad: *"You better watch what you say, those teachers work hard to help you and you just give them trouble!"*
>
> Todd usually came back with: *"Dad, you don't know, they don't care about me. They're just there for their paycheck!"*

Dad: *"Well, you'd better listen to them if you want a*
       paycheck of your own someday." (The argument is
       a destructive one, each looking for weaknesses in
       the other. There are no winners and no progress but
       there is a little entertainment for Todd.)

Todd said he didn't like these arguments, but that's question-
able because he always came back for more. As a matter of fact,
his mother told me, *"I just don't get it. Todd deliberately stirs up
his Dad."*

Of course, Todd had no intention of being insulting to teachers. That was too dangerous. He just talked about being insulting,
maybe as a way of getting out some frustration, and then later as a
way of stirring up a little excitement at home. Being only ten,
**Todd might not even know he has a habit of putting down
teachers at home, and no idea at all as to why he does it.** If
Todd's parents want a change, they need to work with the behavior
in front of them not the threat of what he does, or might do, at
school.

We need new topics for Todd and his dad to talk about, and
they must be worked out in advance. If Dad can be ready with
good topics, he and Todd won't be so easily drawn into new verbal
fencing matches.

With new topics and Dad on the alert for chances to compliment and encourage Todd for any good behavior, the family
airways will improve. **Some of the best rules for parents are the
ones that put them on the alert to see and react to the best
behavior of their children.**

Helping a Child Explore
Alternatives to a Problem

Reflecting a child's statements can help get him or her to a point of exploring alternatives and taking action to solve a problem. It helps when a parent sends the messages, *"I heard you"* and *"It's all right to feel the way you do."* Then your son or daughter is likely to risk talking about possible answers to questions like: *"What can I do about it?"* or *"What would help?"* A parent helps most by tuning in to the child's level of feeling and energy for the problem.

Is the child looking for alternatives, considering a particular one, or just letting out emotion? All of these purposes are good. The parent must listen with empathy and react appropriately to give support. If the child is just venting emotion, a helpful parent reflects that and does not give or push the child to look for answers.

Lori:	*"Mr. Factors is a terrible math teacher! He won't even let you ask a question."*
Mom:	*"That's important in math—to get the problems straightened out before going on."*
Lori:	*"Sure. How can I learn if he won't answer the questions?"*
Mom:	*"Does he ever review?"*
Lori:	*"Oh, sure, he reviews, but it's so fast nobody knows what he's talking about."*
Mom:	*"Why don't you go in after class?"* (Whoops, Mom just took a little superior view here. Lori may not be ready for advice. Let's give Mom a second chance.)
Mom:	*"Why does he go so fast?"*

Lori: *"Who knows? What a jerk."* (Lori's voice is
          lower now, running out of steam for this topic.)
Mom: *"Some teachers are hard to deal with."*

You may feel a little impatient with Mom in this conversation. Why doesn't she help? Couldn't she at least encourage her to go in after class? Or encourage her to speak up insistently in class?

If this is the third complaint about Mr. Factors, Mom might give some of that advice, but I think on the first round she should pass up the temptation to give advice and just let her daughter know she's on her side. How can her daughter feel comfortable and spontaneous in bringing up topics and venting some steam if Mom always makes the talk into a project to fix something?

> *An offer of help, especially too early, can be offensive because it's a message that says, "You don't know. Let me take over."*

Parents love to fix things, especially quickly! **Parents, particularly fathers it seems, can be too efficiency-oriented in their conversations with kids.** If you told someone you had trouble tying your shoe this morning, would you want them to tell you how to do it? No. As a matter of fact, it would be an insulting implication that you are a complete klutz!

So venting frustration is not necessarily a call for help. Remember kids are always on the lookout for what the conversation is saying about them! An offer of help, especially too early, can be offensive because it's a message that says, *"You don't know. Let me take over."*

Here's another child, Dan, complaining for the fifth time about some obnoxious playmates. He's gone by the blowing-off-steam stage. The comment coming up is an indirect request for some help. The help he gets from Mom is a review of alternatives *he* suggests. If that doesn't work, and he asks for more help, she will give her own advice.

> Dan: *"I don't know what to do!"*
>
> Mom: *"What alternatives are there?"* (Children are creative at listing options when they are ready. But if nothing comes up, the problem may not be clear yet and Dan needs to explore more or just express more opinions and feelings. Perhaps he's ready to try an alternative.)
>
> Dan: *"I'm going to tell those kids to quit bugging me!"*
>
> Mom: *"How do you think they'll react to that?"*
>
> Dan: *"They might stop, but if they don't I'll just ignore them from now on."*
>
> Mom: *"Just ignore them?"*
>
> Dan: *"Yeah, that works every time!"*

Well, it might not work every time, but at least Dan is in control and working on his own problem. Distinguishing different levels of emotion and energy and reacting with the right amount of support requires practice and empathy from the parent. When in doubt, be reflective and use "it" questions, but resist the temptation to suggest solutions.

Suggesting Solutions

Parents are always tempted to suggest solutions to problems: *"Why don't you . . ."* *"You should try. . ."* *"Don't be so . . ."* These statements are well-meaning, but they often strike the listener as being pushy and superior. So in addition to avoiding criticism by using "it" questions and reflective statements, we need to add another guideline: **Use statements that suggest solutions**

carefully, and only after all of the problem has been fully expressed.

The purpose is to have the child explore for alternatives, not to have the parent suggest solutions. As an example, look at the temptations in the following conversation:

> Mary: *"Life is so depressing. People are so bad."*
> Mom: *"I know it gets like that at times."*

Here's a good start. It may seem like a terrible start because of the topic, but the topic is Mary's choice. A terrible start would be for Mom to fall to temptation and disagree right away by saying: *"You shouldn't talk like that; there are a lot of good people in the world!"*

It would be tempting to make this correction immediately, but it's unnecessary. Mary knows her remark is extreme. Also it would be a little dishonest on Mom's part because she knows Mary is partly right. Since it's a statement with some potential for agreement, Mom takes the side that puts her a little closer to Mary. Let's see how it goes:

> Mary: *"It gets like that <u>all</u> the time at school."*
> Mom: *"There must be some times that are good at school."*

Not good. It's too early in the conversation for the implied disagreement, authority, and solution expressed in this nudge. Let's let Mom take that back and try again:

> Mom: *"School's been bad lately, huh?"*

This is better because it's reflective, not argumentative, and without evaluation of who's to blame. It keeps the conversation focused on a third entity where Mary started it (not her fault; not Mom's). The next remark from Mary is likely to be informative about what the problem is at school. If Mom continues to "lay back," she will learn a great deal and Mary will have the chance to "get it all out."

In most conversations between adults, the suggestions for solutions are completely left out. You don't often end up a conversation with your neighbor: *"So we're agreed you'll cut the hedge at least every two weeks"* or, *"So don't go roaring off in your car like that; it disturbs everyone."* With these reactions you would never see your neighbors!

Be satisfied that most conversations with your child, like those with your neighbor, will have little result. Leave out the closing comment in most of your conversations. If you try to be the "winner" in every talk then you will also be making a "loser." Frequent "losers" will want to avoid the "game" altogether.

Discuss TV's Content to Practice the Rules of Conversation.

Children and parents need variety from the daily routine and from repetitious topics: friends, school, and hobbies. When Mom and Dad look for topics they can discuss with their sons or daughters, TV programs often show up on the list. Many parents may see TV as an intruder to parental influence. But in small amounts, it can be a rich source of neutral, lively subjects for conversation, especially when adults and children watch together.

Dad: *"What did you think of that show?"*

Lisa: *"The babies stole the audience! They were cute."*

Dad: *"Never cried or needed diaper changes."*

Lisa: *"Not very realistic, I guess, but I liked Grandpa talking to the twins."*

Dad: *"Babies need to hear a lot of talk to learn."*

TV situations are not threatening because they happen to someone else, and the child has as much information as the parent because both watched the same show. Help your child react to and question TV shows, instead of simply letting him/her be a passive viewer. Examples of the social skills and other learning of the next three chapters will come up in TV discussions. You have your attitudes and answers to life's questions, and TV, a *little* TV, can help your child form his/her views, especially with someone there who listens and asks questions.

Children Imitate

A caution about watching TV: Monitor your children's TV viewing closely. What are they watching? Too often situation comedies show family interactions made of sarcasm, put-downs and lack of respect for all family members.

And how many murders are committed each day on TV? As if that alone wasn't bad enough, the killing is seen as an ordinary part of life, and the killers act without care, feeling or remorse.

One father told me that his five-year-old daughter was using the word "hate" frequently, and he was wondering why. Watching her favorite cartoon show gave him the answer. He found that the word "hate" was used again and again and that the only large, adult-like (parent-like) figure was the enemy of all the little people in the cartoon.

11
Coaching Social Skills

Why are some children likable? Is it all appearance
and "personality?" No. We parents know that being
"likable" is also made up of specific behaviors. It's
a matter of showing some genuine unselfish liking
of others. People with this attractive habit are not
only likable but also are often imitated by the
people around them.

Another Crucial Growing Up Question:
"Mom, How Can I Get the Kids to Like Me?"

What a heart-breaking question! Can a parent provide any real
help to a child with this worrisome problem? Yes, specific practical suggestions can make a difference. Jason has a good social
habit of an occasional question:

Jason: *"So, Joey, how did your soccer game go?"*
Joey: *"What? Oh, it was OK."*

Jason: *"Must have been a mess with all that rain."*
Joey: *"Yeah, you should have seen the mud down at the goal. Our goalie looked like a pig!"*
Jason: *"Our field still had some grass down there."*
Joey: *"Did you have to play that Kickers team?"*
Jason: *"Yes. Have you played them already?"*

Most adults know this part of getting along and remember to express some genuine unselfish interest and liking for others.

Children and teens can be cynical and believe that being "likable" is "inborn" and each of us must suffer with our inherited "personality." But most adults have seen a low responder like Joey "brighten up" or "turn around" with a compliment or question that shows interest in his life. How responsive and "attractive" Joey is can change. It depends on his companions *and his own effort.*

Jason's attractive habit is often imitated and Joey, not usually outgoing, picks up the topic and finally has a question of his own. Jason partly creates his own pleasant social world. Both Jason and Joey probably like each other because of the social habits they "draw out" of each other.

Being "Likable" is More than Asking Questions

Just asking a few questions will not turn a person's social life around. So after making a little effort by asking some questions, children and teens will still often keep appearance first on the "Likable Characteristics List" followed by clever, cool, or funny conversation in second place.

The characteristic missing from the list usually shows up when the child or teen is asked who *he* likes. Usually, the answer is that he likes people who accept him, admire him, and want to spend time with him! Sometimes the view from the other person's perspective leads to the discovery that: *"To be liked, I should make an effort in my social habits and not be too critical."* This would include the habit of asking about the other person and showing concern, complimenting, and giving time and companionship. These are the reactions to look for when trying to teach a troubled child about being "likable."

Being a Friend or Being a Critic

The first social difficulty for a young child is usually frequent fighting, grabbing or crying as a result of not understanding how to cooperate with someone else. For the difficult child, it either goes his way and he ignores the cooperative behavior of others (there's no problem when I get what I want!) or it doesn't go his way and he tries to punish the offending companion. Such a "me first" child is usually the first one that other children, teachers, and parents complain about.

The times and places of play are the first opportunities to practice successful social behavior. They also may show a parent the first need a child has to learn the difference between *cooperation* with a companion and the *criticism* characteristic of a competitor. Many troubled marriages include a spouse who is unable to make this distinction!

A young child, or a father for that matter, looking to satisfy his own wants, may not understand that his expression of friendship, or his challenge of competition, is immediately reflected back to him in the reactions of those around him.

> *A child has to learn the difference between <u>cooperation</u> with a companion and the <u>criticism</u> characteristic of a competitor.*

Adults who must supervise children with little or no social skills usually try to present a good model of partnership and discourage competitive attitudes. They keep reprimands to the minimum. This can be a good strategy if the infrequent reprimands are very specific and the positive modeling is done frequently.

It seems natural to the adult to target some deserving child for friendly attention and hope that the other more troublesome child will imitate the adult. Unfortunately, the troublesome child usually thinks his needs have priority over learning social skills. So the adult behavior to be modeled will need to be presented frequently to our problem kid. We will also have to catch him being good at something in order to support him and to show him the way to get along with others and be likable.

Sociability

One mom described the difference between her daughters to me this way: *"Dianne and her sister Kelly are so different.* **Kelly can't stop talking and Dianne hardly says a word. It's hard to believe they were raised in the same family!**

"Last week, I took them to a neighborhood birthday party and when I asked them how it went, Kelly said, 'It was great! They dropped all these balloons on us and everyone screamed! Sally was there, Ann was there, Betty, Millie, and all the boys, Frank, Donald, David and Cris.'"

When Mom asked Dianne how it went she just said that, *"It was OK. Everyone was running all over."* But Kelly said Dianne just stood around.

Being sociable is like many other activities: If you're good at it, you like it, and you tend to get more practice. On the other hand, if you don't socialize easily, then you will have less practice, fewer chances to learn social skills, and the cycle continues.

Kelly's focus is on others; she asks a lot of questions and

remembers a lot of details that she is forever talking about. Dianne's concern is for her own security. She can't seem to think of anything safe to say. Both girls have habits that per- petuate their attitudes. Kelly talks a great deal, she is loud, and she has learned about the other kids. Dianne doesn't talk much, she uses a soft voice, and her lack of experience with others leaves her short on subjects to bring up.

> *Being sociable is like many other activities: if you're good at it, you like it, and tend to get more practice.*

Dianne doesn't have a "problem." She has a quiet style which sometimes makes her feel left out, but she shouldn't be given the extra burden of being told she has some- thing wrong with her.

Her parents could give her some extra social ammunition when going into a social situation. Adults help each other with this kind of priming quite often: *"Remember* (Mom says on the way to her office party with Dad) *my boss, Jane, has that little boat out on the town lake, and she just got back from Florida. Tom bought a car just like ours, and Harold Teak's daughter just made him a grand- father."*

These little bits of information will allow Dad to "go more than half-way" in starting a conversation with Mom's co-workers, if he wants to. Dianne needs some help with information too. She may complain that *"No one came over to me at the party,"* but the parental reflex of *"Did you go over to any of them?"* could be omitted. Instead, before the party, Mom and Dad might give Dianne whatever information might help her.

Dad doesn't get a lecture on how to correct some defect in himself on the way to Mom's party, he's just provided with a better chance of doing what he wants to do with information about the others. And Dianne doesn't need more criticism either, just some long-term help as the situations come up. If she is inclined to join in the talk, thinking of a topic will be easier.

A child who is good at socializing has many friends; they agree on what they want to do, laugh at the same things, and cooperate on the same tasks. They don't seem to try to please each other, they just do.

The notion of being pleasing in order to get along with others may seem a bit simple-minded and of little use until pleasing, agreeing, disagreeing, fighting and cooperating are seen as special cases of social rewards and punishments. Consider, for example, the following conversation I heard when visiting a first-grade art class. It took place at a table where three boys were working on pictures.

Eddie:	(Pokes Tom) *"Don't do it like that, Dum-Dum!"*
Tom:	*"Leave me alone!"*
Jon:	*"Give me the yellow."*
Eddie:	(Reaches for the yellow crayon and pulls it close to himself.) *"I need it now."*
Teacher:	*"Eddie, give Jon the yellow crayon."* (Eddie throws the crayon at Jon.)

Later Eddie turns to Jon.

Eddie:	*"Are you through with the yellow now?"*
Jon:	*"Yes."* (As Jon starts to hand over the crayon, Eddie grabs Jon's hand and digs out the crayon.)

What are the special cases of reward and punishment during this art lesson? First, Eddie punished Tom (*"Don't do it like that, Dum-Dum"*). Second, Tom tried to punish Eddie (*"Leave me alone!"*). Third, Eddie refused Jon's request for the crayon and later added another punishment by snatching it back from Jon.

Eddie was a punisher. He looked for things to punish, and if he didn't find them, he would punish good behaviors of others (Jon's offer of the crayon, for example). **The best way to avoid punishment from Eddie, perhaps the only way, is to avoid Eddie!**

Eddie creates his own social world and probably finds that other children, and people in general, react negatively to him. **He models punishment for others and receives punishment from those who are copying him or who just want to even the score.**

> *Ignoring bad behavior has to have the companion effort of, "catch 'em being good."*

For Eddie to learn a new social style, someone will have to reward Eddie for any little acceptable response, and that person will have to be a good model as well. It's a tough assignment for a parent. The reflex reaction to such a nasty child is to react in kind, but Eddie's mom will need to learn to watch for Eddie's infrequent successes and coach his social game by encouraging the rare moments when he acts properly.

Eddie's mother will also have to provide as little attention as possible when he punishes others. If he uses verbal abuse, she might try ignoring all but the worst of it. But remember that ignoring has to have the companion effort of "catch 'em being good!"

There is no quick fix to Eddie's problem, and we'll have to settle for small successes in the midst of some not very pleasant situations. With close attention Eddie's parents might find that certain situations are better than others. Eddie's fatigue, hunger, or time when his parents are busy may indicate the worst moments. Perhaps family times after meals before Eddie is too tired may be the best times to look for good Eddie-behavior to encourage. These good moments might be the most effective time for his parents to show a good example as well.

The (Social) Games Children Play

"Don't play games with me!" an aggravated parent will say. But everyone plays a few games and the best step toward dealing with them is made when the parent recognizes a game and the way to end it.

Game 1: "Referees Are Fun"

Steven: *"Mom! Mark won't let me watch my program!"*

Mom: *"Mark, let your brother alone. Steven gets to watch his program now."*

Mark: *"It's a dumb program and we can see the last of it later. I'm turning it to my show!"*

Steve: *"Mom! Mark changed the channel!"*

Mom: *"Mark, you come out here and help me and leave Steven alone!"*

Mark: *"Steven tripped me!"*

Steven: *"Mom, Mark pushed me!"*

Mark: *"I have to get around you! Mom told me to go out there, so I have to push!"*

Mom: *"You two cut that out! Mark get out here right now! If I have to come in there..."*

In this game, Mom is referee—the third party the kids go to for judgment calls, penalties, and control of the game. It's safer than regular conflict because you can count on Mom to call a halt to the escalation. By the way, as all Little League and soccer mothers know, referees are always wrong for 50% of the players. **So if you lose you can always blame the referee—what a comfortable way to pass some time!**

Why don't adults play this game? Sometimes they do, of

course. It's just that the third party referee can't be counted on to keep the game going or to intervene when the conflict gets hot. Once the referee leaves the game or fails to play the role of protector, the players have to quit or start negotiating.

Most referees are tempted to coach now and then and parents are no different: *"Mark, why don't you let Steven watch his program and then you can watch yours. Then tomorrow at this time you will get to choose."* Being a coach or arbitrator is more comfortable for a parent than being a referee who gives penalties and gets blamed for everything wrong.

If the suggested solution is rejected, Mom could always end the game by removing the source of the argument. She could turn off the TV. The danger here is that one of the combatants may like that outcome. So calling off the game needs a promise that neither side can have the TV for their half of the time until agreeing to Mom's solution.

The resolution here can't be perfect for the kids. But the goal here is to get Mom out of the referee role. The "less-than-perfect" solution can be fixed any time the brothers want to fix it. Many of these games become much less troublesome to parents when they identify the game and adjust their reactions. Instead of controlling the game and trying to make everyone happy, they just remove or change their role in it.

Game 2: "I'll Bet You Can't Make Me Happy"

Here is a game that also pulls the parents into the problems of their children when the children should be taking responsibility for themselves.

Lynn:	*"Mom, what can I do, I'm bored."*
Mom:	*"Why don't you work on your puzzle?"*

> Lynn: *"I've done everything but the sky part, and that's too hard."*
> Mom: *"Well, how about helping me outside?"*
> Lynn: *"That's just work."*
> Mom: *"Well, you might as well get your homework done."*
> Lynn: *"I don't have to do it yet"*
> Mom: *"Well, why don't you…"*

Many parents recognize this conversation as one that could go on and on. There's a little attention from Mom as long as no suggestion is right. As a matter of fact, if a suggestion were accepted, the game would be over. Suppose old hard-headed Uncle Harry and his friend, Al, came over and started this game with you? **You would probably make a few suggestions, and then since they are adults, you would think it was time for the old coots to entertain themselves.**

Parents can't win the "I-bet-you-can't-make-me-happy" game, they just have to make a reasonable suggestion and then quit and let children get some experience taking control of their own time.

Game 3: "My Problem Is Your Problem"

This is a common children's game that will develop later in teenage years into *"It's your fault because you're my parent(s)."* **As with many of these games, frankly stating the fair truth may stop the game and allow some real progress.**

> Sam: *"This homework is due tomorrow!"*
> Mom: *"Well, you'd better get at it."*
> Sam: *"Where's some paper?"*
> Mom: *"In the desk."*

Sam: *"I already looked there."*

Mom: *"Why don't you try upstairs?"*

Sam: *"Mom! It's supposed to be down here! Could you go look?"*

Mom: *"Hold it, Sam, your homework is your responsibility; don't make it my problem."*

This game has a little of the flavor of the "I'll-bet-you-can't-make-me-happy" game. In both cases parental attention looks suspiciously like the reward that's prolonging the game, and it's time to put Sam on his own for awhile to search for his own solutions.

Game 4: "You're the Parent, Let Me Tell You Your Job"

Ray: *"I'd like to take those self-defense classes, Dad."*

Dad: *"Good exercise. And it could come in handy."*

Ray: *"Well, the ones I want to take are in Freetown."*

Dad: *"Freetown? That's almost an hour from here."*

Ray: *"Sam is in the one here and I don't like him."*

Dad: *"I can't drive two hours every Saturday because you don't like Sam."*

Ray: *"You're supposed to help me. There's no other way."*

Dad: *"You could take the lessons here."*

Ray: *"You're the Dad. You're supposed to take me!"*

Dad: *"Ray, I'll be glad to take you to the lessons here, but I have a life on Saturdays, too. I'm not driving to Freetown."*

Ray's game brings up the important notion that Dad has the right to be selfish at times. Ray's tactic of telling Dad what his responsibilities are isn't working and he may change the game to:

Game 5: "If You Serve Me, I Won't Make You Feel Guilty"

Ray: *"David's father drives him to Freetown."*

Dad: *"Well, I don't have that much time."*

Ray: *"Time for your own son?"*

Dad: *"Ray, don't start that. You know I spend a lot of time with you on our projects."*

Well, this is not going well for Ray and if he doesn't think of a good argument fast, he's going to have to take lessons locally. Ray may have to start yet a new game:

Game 6: "I'm Not Responsible, You Are Guilty for My Mistakes"

Ray: *"Well, don't blame me if I get in a fight with Sam."*

Dad: *"What?"*

Ray: *"You're making me take the lessons here, so if I get into trouble it's your fault."*

Dad: *"Ray, you are responsible for what you do. If the situation with Sam is that bad, maybe you should skip the lessons."*

Ray is almost out of ammunition for this argument and is in danger of having to show responsibility and some consideration for Dad. He can't have his own way, and like the rest of us, he resents having to compromise and make some extra effort to get along. What tactic is left?

Game 7: "You're Not Right, Because...Because"

Ray: *"Dad, it's not that far over there."*
Dad: *"It's the other side of the interstate!"*
Ray: *"The lessons here are not as good."*
Dad: *"You haven't tried any yet."*
Ray: *"They might cost more money here."*
Dad: *"Call and find out."*

Is Ray going to agree now? Probably not. After asking Dad to make the call, bringing up Sam again, and getting out a map to show Dad he's wrong, he may call. Then, if Dad agrees on the price, he may start the lessons when he realizes Dad is not going to Freetown. The key here is Dad's firmness for his own welfare without attacking Ray with, *"You're inconsiderate, irresponsible, selfish, etc."* Dad sticks to the issues, not Ray's personal traits.

Game 8: "If You Really Loved Me, You Would Serve Me"

Here's a game similar to the *"my-problems-are-your-problems"* game with an extra pull on the guilt strings of Dad or Mom.

Ralph: *"Dad, I need those shoes!"*
Dad: *"Ralph, I told you. You have a pair of running shoes. One pair is enough."*
Ralph: *"But these are different. Ed's dad got him a pair."*
Dad: *"I said one pair is enough. It costs too much money."*
Ralph: *"Ed's dad said they're worth it for his son!"*
Dad: *"Ralph, don't run that guilt trip on me. I'm the guy who bought you the first pair, remember?"*

Calling Ralph on his attempt to blame his dad for his troubles will not stop this argument, but when Dad recognizes the game, he can keep the proper view of the talk and not let the son get control of his father's emotions.

The reason for game-playing could be disguised. Possibly some chain or group of behaviors is performed before the child gets what he wants. For example, complaining about school only results in the parents' suggestion on what to do about homework, which gives an opportunity for procrastination about it and then the game begins.

The complaint is a step along the way to the child's goal. Consider the child who fights and complains about his siblings in order to get his parent to referee and then separate them. He now has a short entertainment of "Referees are fun" followed by the room to himself.

Listening During the Game

Good parental listening skills are crucial to handling the games that children play. When the conversation starts, look at your son or daughter rather than a TV screen or newspaper. To deal with a game you need all of your attention on it. Turn and face him or her so that there is no impression that you will miss what's really going on. These physical features of your attention let him or her know that you're paying attention and are not likely to be fooled by a game.

Reflecting back what your child just said is a good habit during these conversations. Let him know that you heard what he said by repeating it. Avoid suggesting solutions in these games, they only lead to "make-me-happy" or "my-problem-is-yours." Also, suggesting solutions makes you sound superior and tempts your child to counter with something different just to stay even.

Take up the habit of asking questions in a form that is not threatening. Don't try to "win." Parents who frequently try to win by getting their son or daughter to *say* they'll try harder, be more responsible, or not be bad any more, may feel some progress has been made. But every time you make a winner you have to make a loser and the next conversation is likely to be more confrontational as the child tries to improve his record.

12
Coaching Special Behaviors

Babies seem totally dependent, and it follows that parents will be in total control. But new parents soon realize that complete control was never possible. They can't control their baby's fidgeting and restlessness. Hunger, fatigue, and the need for an occasional diaper change just happen to the child with little control by anyone. These three basics—eating, sleeping, and toilet training—need special thoughtful strategies.

As babies grow into toddlers and into the attention-getting stage, parents can have a little more direct influence because parents *are* the source of attention.

After the attention-getting stage, children develop additional needs for the social skills of the previous chapter and the school skills coming up in Chapter 13. At these later stages, outside influences increase and as the teenage years approach many parents feel relegated to a coaching role on the sidelines of their child's life. Meeting the needs of babies, toddlers, and older children requires a lot of parental planning, so let's start with the basics.

The Basic Three:
Eating, Sleeping, and Toilet Training

The basic three are in troublesome territory because parents have limited control and information about the real moment-to-moment needs of the child, and a strong desire for everything to go well for the sake of their child's health. The three are such natural and necessary behaviors you would think they would be the easiest for parents to teach and children to learn but that's not always so.

Since almost all adults end up learning the basic three, we know the job is eventually accomplished. Why is it, then, that the basic three are often the basic troubles for parents?

As all experienced parents know, eating, sleeping, and elimination have special characteristics beyond just getting energy, rest and essentials for health. Here are six aspects of the basic three to keep in mind.

1. The basic three are somewhat out of the control of parents—you can't directly force someone to eat, sleep, or use the bathroom.

2. The only direct information about the moment-to-moment need for food, sleep, or elimination comes from the child and is not directly observable by parents.

3. The behaviors are somewhat out of the control of the child as well as the parent. Other conditions, deprivations and feelings enter in. A child cannot feel hungry on demand or sleep any time the request comes up.

4. The basic three are partly driven by even more obscure conditions, experiences and habits that may seem irrel-

evant. Even with us adults, our eating, sleeping, and
bathroom activities are related, in a way not completely
understood, to coffee, tea, excitement, boredom, depression, too little or too much exercise, the need to escape an
unpleasant situation or thought, or worries and fears—just
to name a few.

5. Cultural taboos are emphasized in the basic three. Mistakes
here produce the most wrath, embarrassment, and guilt.
Under that pressure, children learning the basic three are
somewhat at the mercy of uncontrollable conditions and
squeezed by the emotional pressures. Parents can help by
controlling daily experiences, diet, and deprivations, but
rules with consequences must be handled very carefully
with the basic three because it is tempting to make demands
on children who are too young or too upset. With children
who may not be developed enough to perform, the risks of
mistakes, disappointments and lasting confrontations are
very high.

6. Being private activities, the basic three also comprise the
last bastion of control over one's own life and it's the last
place we tolerate interference. One theory of anorexia
(refusal to eat) is that the person needs to prove some
control over at least part of her life. As one daughter with
an eating disorder said to me, *"They* (parents, relatives,
teachers, and nearly everyone else) *tell me what to wear,
when to wear it, when to get up, play, work, and go to bed.
But they can't make me eat. At least I control that! And
I'll prove it, I won't eat anything!"*

Eating

Children can eat or not eat for fun, adventure, attention, "control" of the situation, or to "win" in a power struggle with Mom or Dad. For the most common family situations, a parent's most promising strategy is just engineering the environment.

The engineering the environment strategy should be similar to the same limits we have for the adults in the household. Eating is limited to what is in the house and provided at the table, leaving the choices as much as possible to the person. It's better to take control where you have it—during the food shopping. Instead of bringing home a gallon of ice cream and then practically needing a refrigerator lock or dog-leash to keep the kids from eating it, you're better off not buying it.

Left to their own judgment, most children will select a good diet overall but will also make plenty of mistakes, deviating from what is good for them along the way—the same pattern you find in us adults. To highlight this area of behavior when there's no real problem is to tread on dangerous territory for no good reason.

> *Take control where you have it—when you are food shopping.*

Many families report that mealtimes highlight their biggest complaints. The atmosphere there extends into other family activities so any extra unjustified confrontation is not in the best interest of the family.

If you are going to use a tougher rule about eating, you need to be sure that the goal is worth the effort, and that the performance required is well within range of your daughter's (or son's) abilities. Maybe the rule (to eat *all* food served) is too big a step and one not even required of adults. Possibly we need an easier rule with the choices limited by what is available.

You could decide that your daughter can't have dessert until she's finished the food on her plate, but this might be ineffective if she is allowed snacks later while watching TV. But allowing alternative freebies is no sin unless it weakens the usefulness of an important rule. You might remove these alternative freebies and find that your daughter still does not care about the dessert option.

> *If you are going to use a tougher rule about eating, make sure the goal is worth the effort.*

You should look carefully at the rule and the level of performance it requires. The goal is for the child to recognize and satisfy his or her own hunger with what's available. If parental demands and arguments insist on too much control, the child may ignore her own body cues of hunger and the stage is set for trouble.

Sleeping

Sleeping problems can be a whole different level of anxiety for parents. While many adults hold easily to a sleeping pattern, it is usually an individual pattern with frequent variations from week to week.

A child deserves the same flexibility. Painful as it may be to delay bedtime after a full day of demanding parenting, the fact is that a child's need for sleep is still a product of many variables. However, if bed, bedtime, and isolation in the bedroom have not been used in negative negotiations during the day, sleeping will be welcomed at least as often as it is for adults.

The cautions on using sleeping, naps, and bedtime as a time-out are discussed in Chapter 9. Usually the price to be paid at bedtime is too much.

A child's unpredictable bedtime behavior may be a problem

only in the mind of the parent and then developed from the parental reactions into a larger problem. Better to look first at the diet and exercise that create the need for sleep. Snacks and drinks just before bed are a particularly important part of the diet related to sleep.

Establish a pleasant routine of bathing and reading. Then use the routine regularly, letting the time of the routine vary as needed. Snacks and caffeine from a glass of coke or chocolate milk can disturb the sleep of a 150-pound adult; think how concentrated that amount is in a small child!

Perhaps another behavior chart from the exercise of T-1 (page 28) is in order here. Drinks particularly those with sugar or, please forbid it, caffeine, should be recorded in the behavior chart along with time of day, other food, the day's exercise, and the discussion of problems and worries in the evening. Also add a place in the chart for TV, both amount and type.

Look first at the diet and exercise that create the need for sleep.

Determining what plays a role in your child's sleep pattern is your best hope for a satisfactory one.

Since sleep problems can be influenced by exercise and naps during the day, the behavior chart on sleep should include these activities.

So the first point is not to approach the problem as if it could be influenced by consequences at bedtime, but rather as if it could be influenced by other behaviors and conditions of the day under the control of the parents.

Toilet Training

Most psychologists consider toilet training a crucial childhood experience. Theories back to Freud and before him have discussed the symbolic nature of the behavior. In the practical situation, toilet training acquires some of its importance from the natural reaction of parents to the disgusting outcomes of mistakes. **The emotions are in the nature of the parent and not yet the child.**

Be comforted by the fact that nearly everyone arrives at adulthood having learned this behavior despite all the parental concern and anxiety about toilet training. Very few children make it to four without great progress in this area. Mistakes occur all the way to the teens when the "child" is distracted or excited, but regardless of the method, we parents have about 100% success in this area—not something we can say about all the projects in this book! **The promise of this inevitable success should be a great comfort and can allow parents to remain calm when mistakes happen.**

> *Be comforted by the fact that nearly everyone arrives at adulthood having learned this behavior.*

Starting toilet training too soon will produce many mistakes and disappointments because this behavior is not controllable by the parent and may not yet be controllable by the child. An early start in this area creates the risk of bigger problems and confrontations later.

The mistakes produce the emotion, so it would be best to maximize the possibilities of rewards for success. First, you need a behavior chart to put by the diaper pail. Write in the hours of the day across the top and note every time a diaper goes into the pail. Label a row for each day and leave a space for remarks.

Using 1's and 2's for wet and dirty diapers can give you some notion of when the best time for training would be. When the

numbers collect at certain times of the day, you have an indication
of when training is likely to be successful. If "accidents" are still
happening at all times of the day, it's not time to start.

**When the training begins, continue your chart to note
successes and reward the child.** The best reward will be your
reaction, but you may want to include a treat for success. At first
you'll need to give encouragement
just for staying on the toilet. Later, the
rewards can come for successes.

> *Keep the praise up,*
> *the emotion down,*
> *and the tolerance high.*

If there has already been some
emotion over this training and your
child is resisting, you may need to
start with a new situation and gradually move the training back to
the bathroom. For example, you might begin by rewarding your
child for sitting on a portable potty in the bedroom, then the hall,
then the bathroom. Keep the praise up, the emotion down, and the
tolerance high. Remember that all the adults you know eventually
learned this, and you don't have to meet anybody's schedule here.

Bed-Wetting: Occasional bed-wetting is normal for children
under the age of 10. Beyond 10, pull-ups or big-child diapers may
have to serve as a temporary solution. But frequent bed-wetting
can be a medical problem because certain infections of the bladder
and urinary tract produce uncontrolled urination.

The first place to start on this problem is at your physician's
office. When you are sure that a physical ailment is not the problem, you could use a bed-wetting alert device which is usually very
successful. This device consists of two pads of metal foil separated by a plastic fiber lining. The three layers are placed under the
bottom sheet of the child's bed. Bed-wetting does not begin
abruptly, so there is time for getting up when **the lining becomes
even a little damp and the alarm buzzer is activated.** At this

stage, the child has time to wake up and go to the bathroom.

Over a few weeks this alarm clock for bed-wetting can teach a child to wake up and use the bathroom. It is battery-operated so there is no danger of shock.

One source for the device is Sears Home Healthcare catalog which can obtained by calling 1-800-326-1750.

Parents must get up with the alarm, too. As with most child-rearing problems, a gadget by itself will not solve problems. You may have to help the child shake out the cobwebs to be awake enough to even *find* the bathroom! A little support for a job well done and you're back to bed without a big event.

The effort is worth it because bed-wetting can complicate other difficulties—fears of sleeping, staying overnight with relatives or friends, embarrassment, and shyness.

The Spoiled Child

Parents usually suspect that some of a child's bad behavior occurs because of the attention it attracts, and their first question should be: *"Why can't my child get the attention he or she needs some other way?"*

Some children may only receive attention and the consideration of the family when they act up. Other children may have developed more pleasing solutions to their attention-getting problem, but if the overall amount of attention drops, they will resort to bad behavior to make up the shortfall. If this strategy works for the child, we might call the child "spoiled."

A "spoiled" child has found a way to control his parents' behavior by punishing them with bad behavior or the threat of it. "Spoiled" is a catch-all term describing many behaviors, some of which may not be bad. The behavior a child uses is usually embarrassing, exasperating, or just plain annoying to the parents. He uses it because it works. Calculated whining and demanding should be handled without saying the child is "spoiled."

The way out of the problem lies in the direction of rewarding the little good behavior there is in a child who may not be very likable or deserving. Added to the "catch 'em being good" rule should be an extinction rule for obnoxious behavior.

> *Calculated whining and demanding should be handled without saying the child is "spoiled."*

Extinction refers to a rule about withholding consequences. In this case, withholding attention and not giving in to obnoxious behavior. Single out one aspect of the "spoiled" behavior and write up an extinction rule about it. For example, if the child begins to cry when he is about to be deprived of something, eliminate the possibility of any change in that decision just because of crying. **Notice the rule in this case singles out crying and does not include any other part of what is called being "spoiled."**

Getting angry, pouting, and other obnoxious behaviors are not part of this rule. For these other behaviors you'll just make your on-the-spot reactions, dealing with the behavior as the situation requires. That on-the-spot decision may include holding to the decision that produced the bad behavior, but the crying rule that says crying is *always* ineffective in getting a reversal still remains.

The reason for this separation of strategies is that an extinction rule is hard to follow and if it is too broad, it will force you to look for too many behaviors at once and consistency will suffer. The small separate rule is more likely to encourage you because any change in the bad behavior highlighted in the rule, in this case, crying, will stand out as a success. Knowing that the extinction rule really works, you have a better chance of holding to the rule in the next situation.

Remember, a spoiled child did not get that way because too much was provided. **Many children in families with small incomes are spoiled, and many children with the benefits of wealthy families are not spoiled.** The routine reactions to acting spoiled determine the child's habit. If obnoxious behavior is "required," then obnoxious behavior is learned.

Some parents have told me that they very carefully avoided giving in to bad behavior, but ended up with a problem child nevertheless. I think many of these parents did, occasionally, avoid supporting bad behavior. Problems developed possibly because consistency was lacking.

Without a clear message about what is right, a child casts around for solutions to his needs and frustrations. What will he find is effective? Over the months and years of growing from a one-year-old to a ten-year-old he will develop his own theory of how to handle life. It may be acting "spoiled," "angry," or "nice." Without much feedback, a child needs only a few unfortunate experiences to become troublesome.

Tracking the Source of Crying and Pouting

These behaviors have something in common: they are directed at the parents. And they are maintained by attention from the parents. But they will go away as the child grows up or at least be replaced by more "adult" manipulations for attracting attention.

Your kitchen chart can come in handy for these behaviors. Keep a record of when the problem occurs and what happened right before and right after the outburst. You may already know that part of the crying is a result of fatigue late in the day or before nap-time. But the crying may also come up for, or be used on, certain members of the family—Mom gets the crying, Dad gets the pouting, for example.

An examination of the chart may show what commonly happens next and a possible change may become obvious. Dad needs to watch his reactions to pouting—even Dad teasing the pouter may be a reward. Mom and Dad need to watch how the child plays them against each other. There may also be a particular circumstance or time of day when bad behavior from the child and mistakes by the parents are most likely.

Many parents find that saying, *"Please use your words, not the crying,"* is a way to help a fussing child.

Behavior During Illness

Every parent knows that a sick child is the source of the most upsetting and helpless feelings in parenthood. This situation changes all the rules. The child needs special care, and all the ground rules of child-rearing change. Everyone wants to make the patient comfortable. With children, particularly, the unusual nature of the situation has to be emphasized because there is a danger of a long-term effect from the illness experience.

We don't want her to learn that special advantages are available whenever she says she is ill. This has the potential to be one of those unfortunate experiences that shape bad social habits in the future. **References to illness are not always verifiable—a headache or upset stomach is a hard claim to check out. Even the child may not be aware that he is exaggerating and using certain claims to control attention from his parents.**

Again, positively stated rules that allow parents to love and attend their child for good reasons are a part of the solution. Also, some of the less attractive but logical consequences of being ill might be emphasized whenever there is reason for suspicion. For example, if a child claims to have a headache and so wants to watch television instead of doing homework, perhaps your first response should be that he lie down and take a nap without TV.

Reasonable reactions should be consistent and prompt to a child beginning to use illness for secondary benefits. If a child says he has a headache, it is probably best to act as if he does. A long argument about whether or not he *really* has a headache only increases the probability that you are giving attention for bad behavior. **But having a headache shouldn't mean that all demands are off and the child gets to do whatever he or she wants.** It should mean acting reasonably to reduce the headache—rest, quiet, and eating only reasonable food.

If you are wondering whether the illnesses are real, set up a chart similar to that described for crying. A record of a week or so might show up some regularities to help sort out illness from false claims.

The "Linus" Syndrome of Thumb and Blanket

Thumb-sucking, like the use of a comforter such as a favorite blanket, serves the purpose of security but can also develop into an attention-getting device. Parents who feel the habit has gone on too long should remember that we all give up our special comforter eventually. So the question is whether or not to hurry the process along.

It takes a little soul-searching to determine whether the problem is with the child or in the mind of the parent. Sometimes parents will say, *"It just bothers me that he (she) is still doing that."* **If the problem is in the mind of the beholder, perhaps it should be dealt with there.**

Breaking the thumb and/or blanket habit is a stressful process at best and may be downright traumatic. If something is to be done, the emphasis ought to be on positive support for activities that require ignoring the blanket and thumb for awhile. Improvement without new emotional problems is almost impossible if discouragement and reprimands for using the comforter are frequent. Usually the child will latch on to some new way of dealing with stress, either choosing to be alone more often or using some defense tactic such as crying, pouting, or throwing tantrums until assured that everything is again under (the child's) control.

> *If the problem*
> *is in the mind*
> *of the beholder,*
> *perhaps it should*
> *be dealt with there.*

Tantrums

When a child who occasionally throws tantrums makes a request, parents need to make a careful decision. **As every parent knows, the decision to deny the request should not be altered by a tantrum. but to avoid the tantrum they are often tempted to give less clear reactions that get them into hot water.**

For example, a request from an explosive child may tempt the parents to put off a confrontation with, *"I'll think about it,"* or *"We'll have to wait until your mother (or father) comes home."* This sets up a long and risky period when a tantrum is likely. For the moment the request has been denied, but it was done in a weak way that tempts the child to fight for what he or she wants—plenty of time to try out a tantrum along with other obnoxious behavior.

Also, putting off the child leaves him with nothing to do for the moment. It takes experience and creativity to put aside one line of activity and take up another while waiting for an answer to come down from the parental powers. Instead of switching to a new activity, the childish thing to do is cling to the present desires and push for closure. **Nagging is followed by complaining, then frustration and attack, and then the whole tantrum.**

Another argument against delayed decisions is that parents

may only resist the early mild tantrums. Such holding out until bad behavior gets worse is certainly a move in the wrong direction. Delays in decisions and giving in to expanding tantrums develop the childish willingness to try to manipulate others by making them miserable.

Fears

One of the major difficulties in dealing with unreasonable fears in children is that adults forget that fears lead to behaviors. They are the result of experience; they are followed by consequences; and they are observed by others. Of course they also exist within the child and they deserve our sympathetic understanding. **So while a parent is sleeping with a frightened child, sitting with one who is afraid of the dark, or carrying a child who is afraid of dogs, a gradual removal of these accommodations needs to be in the plan. But an abrupt, cold turkey approach is not in order.**

Remember that fears are expressed as behaviors but are not necessarily rational and rationality (talking them out of it) will not be very effective. Many fears are conditioned reactions from past traumatic experiences, and this conditioning is not a rational process. If Pavlov's dogs had been rational about conditioning, they would have ignored the bell and saved their spit until the food arrived! Their irrational reaction (salivation) to the bell was not done *in order to* get the food as a reward; salivation just happened because the food was *always* presented after the bell. So even talking dogs would not have been talked out of their "irrational" anticipation of what followed the bell.

The problem of fears calls for a gradual change in the *situation*. For example, fear of the dark will have to start with light which is gradually dimmer or placed farther away. This kind of fading procedure over weeks coupled with lots of support and compliments for small successes can reduce the problem to leaving only a night-light or small table light on. **Talking, threatening, or using the abrupt sink-or-swim technique will only cause terror and distrust.**

Many fears that are viewed as acquired from unfortunate experiences continue because of parental reactions. A child punished by being forced to stay in a room alone or sent to bed may very well come to fear being alone or fear being put to bed. Such punishments can't be undone, but they can give the parent a better understanding of childhood fears and raise concerns about the nature of future punishments.

> _Talking, threatening, or using the abrupt sink-or-swim technique will only cause terror and distrust._

When a specific fear is the problem, we might ask whether the object or situation can be easily avoided. If a child is afraid of the dark, is it OK to leave a light on? The opposite strategy of forcing the child to stay in the dark is usually not effective. Dragging a kicking and screaming child up to a dog in an effort to "get him to understand" that most dogs are nice, only makes him fear _you_ as well as dogs!

Strategies require effort. So the first question to ask about a troublesome behavior is whether or not the problem is serious enough to require attention. If not, then your reactions should be carefully selected to show the appropriate loving sympathy with no additional attention or consequence. Most childhood fears fade away naturally as the result of varying degrees of contact with the feared situation. Parents should keep in mind that time and under-standing are great healers, _if_ there is no attention-getting aspect in the parents' reaction to maintain the fear.

Compulsions and Fidget Behavior

Nail-biting, hair-twirling, nose-picking, and lip-biting are usually maintained partly by parental attention and partly by the absence of something else to do. They are behaviors that fill up time and are occasionally rewarded accidentally by parents.

However, fidget behavior can be more complicated than plain fidgeting. It's fidgeting with a long-term commitment. It happens in the slow, somewhat boring moments of life and almost everyone does it. At first it can be just the random squirming and wiggling of a child. To a child we say, *"Stop that fidgeting!"* Later on, the little habits develop into hair-twirling, scratching, or ballpoint pen-clicking (for us older ones). Even eating and drinking can develop into fidget (fill-up-the-dull-time) behaviors.

A well-known psychology experiment concerning fidget behavior has been repeated many times. A laboratory white rat is trained to press a lever for food. He soon learns that the food is only given after long intervals— about two minutes. In the meantime there is little to do but wait. What to do, what to do? A water bottle is available, but the rat

> *"Jumping on" fidgeting behavior can be a dangerous parental habit.*

has water all the time in his home cage so he is not thirsty. But, faced with nothing to do, he drinks (sound familiar?).

It is not in the rat's nature, or ours, to do absolutely nothing. With humans, doing nothing is even embarrassing. So we pretend to read (or something) in waiting rooms, in restaurants, and at bus stops. Many of us wouldn't go to a restaurant alone without something to read.

So the rat drinks. But not just sips. He may drink up to two times his body weight in water while waiting for time to pass! Since no rat has a bladder that big, you can see that the experiment requires regular cleaning chores.

All that was needed to stop our furry waterholic was to shorten the waiting time—down from 2 minutes to 30 seconds. With the shorter interval all the excess water drinking was gone. Pay-offs came more often, there was work to be done, and our rat had no time for fooling around!

> *If the behavior*
> *is not important,*
> *let's not make it so.*

So now we have *two* possible explana-tions of frequent, repeated, annoying behaviors—one, they could be fidget behaviors to pass the time and, two, they could be attention-getting. The difference is important.

For attention-getting behaviors we need a strategy that reduces the attention for that behavior, but for fidget behaviors we need to reduce the boredom, the down time, the dull moments. Take a little extra time for reflection when you first see the beginnings of a "nervous" habit or a "compulsive" behavior.

Rewarding other behavior that is desirable will be a good strategy in either case, but the reaction to the annoying behavior itself should be a careful one. For attention-getting activities you certainly want to reduce attention, but if it's a fidget behavior, there is all the more reason to see that support and opportunity for more acceptable behavior occurs more often. You wouldn't want to get into a "I'll-bet-you-can't-make-me-happy" game, but clearly some increase in action is called for.

Now that boredom has brought on the behavior, what reward will it attract? "Jumping on" fidgeting behavior can be a dangerous parental habit. If the bad behavior thrives on attention, the parent will need a long remedial strategy later. If the behavior is not important, let's not make it so. Instead let's look to the situation for a way of enriching the moments.

Any smoker or heavy drinker will recognize the fidgeting

aspect of their habit and tell you that the worst time of temptation is during the low moments—not just the depressing ones, but the boring ones, also.

Another strategy for fidget habits is to reward the lack of compulsive behavior. For example, one mother told me she promised a dollar to her son if he could refrain from nail-biting long enough so that his nails would need cutting. **Because this demand seemed a bit too large for a first step, her son was also given a quarter for each one of his fingernails that grew to trimming length.**

Such a direct contingency upon a compulsive behavior must be used carefully. There is always a tendency to do more than just state the rule. Nagging will only ensure that some attention will be connected to mistakes.

Rhythmic Habits

Rhythmic habits are sometimes symptoms of severe childhood disorders. Autistic children often engage in repetitive behaviors for hours and also exhibit developmental disabilities and impairments in mental function.

Normal children and adults have rhythmic habits, too. Tapping a pencil, swinging a foot, and rocking to music are common pastimes. These may annoy parents but are probably too trivial to merit a strategy beyond ignoring.

> *This can be a case of parents trying to fix a non-problem and now they have a problem!*

When the habit has become troublesome, most parents can remember its beginning as a less frequent event. **This can be a case of parents trying to fix a non-problem and now they have a problem!** A behavior that started as just fidgeting became a gimmick for attention, and then a way to express exasperation at the parents. "Getting through to" the parents now gets a reprimand, a kind of attention in a situation where positive attention seems unlikely to the child.

An occasional correction or request to stop the annoying habit is not likely to do much harm if the parent's emotional reaction can be kept in check.

Mom: (Rich has been banging his foot on the chair leg at dinner for three minutes) *"Rich, stop kicking the chair—it's a bother when we're eating."*

Rich: *"I can't help it."*

Mom: (Still in a very quiet tone) *"Well, if you can't help it, you'll have to eat in the small chair with your feet on the floor. Did you finish your picture before dinner?"*

Rich: (Still kicking the chair) *"Yes, it's a boat."*

Mom: *"A boat. I'd like to see it after we're finished. Please don't kick."*

Rich: *"I told you I can't help it."*

Mom: (Still very calmly) *"If you continue, you'll have to be in the little chair. That's one."* (The count-out begins.)

Rich may have to go to three and then to the little chair this first time. Later, if his kicking as a ploy to get Mom going doesn't work, he'll stop or at least keep his excess energy habits at a tolerable level.

Mom is right to provide another direction for Rich's focus. These other topics will have to become a regular part of Mom's habits *before* the chair kicking or other problem starts. **If Mom only comes up with these interests when Rich acts up, you can see where this will lead.**

Taking All That "Guff"

One obvious characteristic of a child's "bad disposition behavior" is that it generally reduces the response of the parent. It's true the parent can silence the child or keep him from acting up by taking a threatening pose that implies punishment. And of course the child learns and uses the same idea, but since he is a less powerful figure he must use it in a more subtle way.

I have named the child's threats and lack of compliance his version of "Guff" or "Guff Control" because some parents I have worked with said they had a habit of giving in rather than "taking all that guff."

Sam uses guff to put his mother off and to get out of some undesirable requests for work. But his behavior also is a result of the fact that the request is *just* work. He is using guff to avoid doing some job because the job itself doesn't pay off.

By this time you may be getting a little tired of the idea that everything has to pay off, but remember that what we mean by "pay off" in many cases is just the honest expression of appreciation, admiration, or support when something good or helpful is done. Material reward is not always necessary. In your job you probably do many things because you have come to believe that it is the right way to do it or that it will please someone. You do not do it necessarily for the money.

Guff control is usually a reaction to too little pay-off. It is continuous because it attracts some attention of its own. Now if it also works in getting out of some requests, we are well on the way to building ourselves a real problem.

Why don't you try guff with your boss? Because it won't work, I would bet. And also with a good boss, it never occurred to you to use guff because there is consistent support for doing the job—pay, appreciation, or some combination of both.

So both Sam and his parents usually engage in some bad disposition behavior or guff. Sam's parents try to bring about some effort from Sam by coercion and Sam avoids that effort, if he can, because it is straight coercion without a significant reward. When Sam is using guff, he often exposes the situation quite well by saying, *"Oh, why should I do that anyway?"* The statement is pure guff intended to stop some request from Mom or Dad, but, incidentally, it asks a very good question: *"What does Sam get out of it?"*

One difficulty is that it is much easier to attempt to coerce some behavior than to plan and provide support for another alternative, as any boss would tell us. Providing reasonable, positive consequences requires planning and sometimes a new point of view that at least includes opportunities for more social approval.

13
Teaching School Skills

Comfort and success in school are crucial ingredients in the happiness of children and parents. The way to this success goes beyond just feeling pride in learning basic skills.

In the first few grades, the most important development is a child's self-confidence and positive expectation for what school has to offer. If you can help your child be comfortable and positive about school, what a gift it is!

And that success not only builds confidence in academic abilities, it influences feelings of competence and usefulness outside of school as well.

Parents of children-turned-students have a new job beyond helping with homework. **Parental advice for good school skills and parental efforts to put the learning to use at home will boost the child's confidence and attitude.**

A Parent's Job Changes as Child Becomes Student

Your first years in school helped shape your early definition of who you were. Comparisons with schoolmates fixed your impression of them and it shaped a judgment of yourself as well, all before you were ten, no doubt. Parents who have attended their own school reunion, after a few years, know how **the reunion seems to measure us against that old bench mark, again. This common reaction to reunions demonstrates how important help in school is to a child.**

We all know the first school days are a big adjustment for the child, but they are also a big adjustment for the parents. It is probably the first time parents are required to share:

1. Child-rearing attitudes
2. The selection of rewards and punishments
3. Control of what will be learned, and
4. Control of daily schedule

This sharing means that other people become important to the child. **Strategies and habits the child developed for dealing with parents might not fit the new people and the new situation.**

Greg: *"Mom, I don't want to go to school any more."*
Mom: *"What? I thought you liked school."*
Greg: *"Well, it's boring and the kids don't like me."*
Mom: *"Getting along in school is hard. What part do you do best?"* (Mom shows good listening in order to hear the whole story.)
Greg: *"Best? Oh, math, I guess, but what good is it anyway? And in geography I just can't remember all that stuff."*

School is such a large part of a child's life that if it isn't going well, it clouds almost all other activities. Greg pointed out several sources of trouble when he said he was bored because he didn't see the use of math, couldn't remember the geography, and "the kids don't like me." Let's start with Greg's boredom.

Providing Answers to "Why Should I Do that Stuff?"

Kids who say, *"It's boring"* **could be sending a confusing message.** They could mean that interest is low, and they don't see the need, or they could mean they are bored because they can't keep up or, the opposite, they are too far ahead. Parents need to sort out these meanings before they react.

The poor student who finds school lessons of "no use" usually means he finds no importance *for him* in the tasks that are requested of him: *"Why should I do that? It's just busy work."* A parent could be misled at this point and start explaining why she, the parent, thinks the work is important.

Mom: *"Math is important, Greg, because one day you'll have to manage your own money and figure out shopping and many other things in life."*

Greg: *"Uh, yeah."*

Mom: *"Also, you need it for the higher math that will get you into college."*

Greg: *"Higher math? There's higher math??? I think I won't go to college."*

Mom: *"Don't talk like that. Of course, you want to go to college."*

The one-day-you'll-need-these-things approach to this problem is not on target with Greg's original objection. His point was that the work is not important *for him.* Greg's value of the "you'll-need-it-for-college" argument is revealed when he suggests giving up college just to avoid math problems tonight!

Mom needs an approach to the meaningfulness and importance of a good education that is within Greg's short-term view of the world. It won't help to provide more arguments about, *"You can't get anywhere without a good education,"* or, *"Jobs will be harder to get, promotions will be harder to come by, and you'll end up with a hard life."*

At the moment, Greg doesn't want, and can't have, those things. The "getting anywhere" idea seems like a probability statement of consequences too far in the future and too abstract. Anyway, the people on TV seem to do all right, some of them without much education, too! How much education would a person need to earn the amount of money that *Greg* would think is plenty?

> *As he learns new things in school each day, he should be encouraged to use his new skills that day.*

So why should Greg study decimals in the fifth and sixth grade? What use is it to know portions of geography or American history? Why are spelling lists important? The answers need to be in the present activities of Greg's life. Remember, he's a person on a short-term priority.

As he learns new things in school each day, he should be encouraged to use his new skills that day. Sometimes that requires some real creativity on the part of the parent. Could Greg use his knowledge of decimals to keep track of the family checking account? Receive a fee for doing so? If we have to drive to visit a friend, could Greg find the route on the map? If we want to leave a note, could Greg write it? If we have to add up the grocery list, could Greg do it? Count out the money? Carry it to the store?

Will he make costly mistakes? Yes. **Couldn't he just stay interested in this stuff until he needs it later on? Probably not.**

One mother I work with shows how such skills are useful by taking her son to the bank with her. She allows him to go in alone and pay the bills. When he returns with the correct change and explains it all, she gives him a "tip."

Of course the tip might not be necessary for many children who would be happy with the importance of the task and trust they were given. The "tip" is a parental judgment call, but **he will never ask why he has to study arithmetic—he knows why.**

> *He's not just a kid, he's a kid with useful skills that his parents respect.*

He also bakes for his mother. And when recipes need to be halved or doubled, she does not interfere in the calculations. From bitter (and sour) experience he knows the importance of these skills. And he feels a little better about his own worth. **He's not *just* a kid, he's a kid with useful skills that his parents respect.**

Many skills not covered in school are also important to learn. Cooking, washing clothes, caring for your room, and later on, car care. All tasks present opportunities for children to learn and gain some feeling of self-esteem as they become competent. The chores may be domestic ones that adults shun or view as burdens. But from a child's view they are, at first, new, and when the novelty has worn off, they still have the potential of letting the child be productive and helpful *now*.

Parents may be called on to show great tolerance as they allow practice with these important school-related tasks or tasks of everyday drudgery that parents could do faster. Calm your impatience with the knowledge that just mastering the task is rewarding to the child, and it insures the further benefit of a little self pride.

Mistakes are easier to tolerate for these activities because the benefit is not only competence but pride. **When the task is closer to drudgery than to adventure, more enthusiastic praise will be needed.**

> *The greatest advantage in teaching is having a student with a reason to learn.*

Ordinarily a person gains little respect and takes little pride in doing drudgery. So when a child asks *"Why should I do this?"* it may be the beginning of an argument but it also signals his need for appreciation for doing the job. For activities that aren't very important, fun, or adult, he's counting on you for support. **His question about drudgery is a cue to focus on encouraging and praising him for a job well done.**

Learning Must Be Useful Now

It's important for parents to provide experiences that point out, here and now, the usefulness of things learned in school. Certainly a 10- or 12-year-old can handle a checking account for the family or plan and carry out the family food shopping. When he/she sits down to do it, you may hear, *"I can't do this because I don't know decimals."* Then you can say, *"Oh, you need to add decimals! Let me go over that with you. Then you can carry on."* Your child may not enjoy the process of learning decimals, but at least now there is a concrete experience of their importance. **The greatest advantage in teaching is having a student with a reason to learn.** When the checking account is balancèd, your child will know the reason for decimals.

For school subjects that do not easily apply to daily tasks, parents can influence their children's respect for the subject by asking questions.

Mom:	*"What did you do in science today?"*
Greg:	*"We numbered the chambers of the heart and followed a drop of blood through the system."*
Mom:	*"I always wanted to know more about that. How does it go through?"*

Show interest in school projects and point out, from news-of-the-day, where knowledge applies. Parent-child conversations that bring in schoolwork show the usefulness of the work and improve Greg's respect for himself.

Another Crucial Growing-Up Question: "How Can I Make the Grade?" (Homework Strategies That Work!)

Greg's second complaint about school showed up in geography. **This time it wasn't so much that he questioned the usefulness of the subject by saying it's "boring" but he found it "boring" because he was not doing well.**

Homework that requires staring at materials and trying to remember can be boring and hard to keep working on. The problem requires a different parental approach:

Greg:	*"I just can't keep the states straight. We're supposed to know them by Friday!"*
Dad:	*"What are they going to ask you about them?"*
Greg:	*"We have to point them out on a blank map with no words or anything."*
Dad:	*"Do you have a map?"*
Greg:	*"I have the one in this book and I've been studying it a lot, but I don't remember much."*
Dad:	*"How do you do the "studying" part?"*

Greg: *"Well, I look at the states and try to remember which ones go where."*

Dad: *"Greg, I think you need to go through a few drills in a situation like the one you're going to have Friday. How about tracing that map so we can have one that's blank like the one you'll see on Friday. Then we'll make a few copies when we go shopping."*

Greg: *"OK, then I could practice by filling in the names on the copies we make."*

Studying requires practice. Greg has been trying to practice in his mind (*"I've been studying it a lot"*), but sitting and staring at a book or homework sheet is not real practice—performance of a behavior—and Greg has not made much progress.

To make homework time successful, Dad first asks Greg what he is *doing*. **Most students who are falling behind don't have a specific target for their effort.** When they study, they stare at things, notes or books. They don't *DO* anything.

Most of us don't have the kind of memory that retains a great deal from just looking; it's the *doing* that will be remembered. What do you remember from your high school days? Spelling? Math and vocabulary you still use (*do* things with)? But I'll bet you remember little of social studies, geography, history, or math you never use.

Reading assignments often lead the student to this mistake of leaving out the *doing* in learning. Many of my students have said, *"I can't believe I did poorly, I went through* (stared at) *all the material for the test!"*

If you only read it (not really practice) and never use it, it will be gone soon. If reading is the assignment, have your student take reading notes, preferably on cards. For each page of reading the student should take some note. *"Never turn a page without writing something,"* should be the rule.

Giving Your Student the Advantage

The reading note requirement has several advantages:

1. It becomes a source of motivation because it is a concrete product from which the student can take a feeling of accomplishment.
2. It is a product that the parent can encourage, review, and use as a basis for other rewards, if that's in the plan.
3. Most importantly, notes provide bench marks of progress that allow the student to pick up at the right place after an interruption. **It's surprising how much studying is done in small sessions of only a few minutes between interruptions by phone calls, snacks, and other chores.** Without a note-taking habit, most of us start again at the same place we started before. With past notes, we have a record of where we are, and we can move on to new material.

A last advantage of active studying comes at review time. A condensation of the work is available as notes, maps, tables, and drill sheets. This will guarantee the right material will be memorized, and you and your student can avoid the time-consuming misery of thrashing madly through unorganized material.

How About a Computer Program to Help Learning?

Computer programs from school or at home can be very helpful, especially if the drills are similar to the other schoolwork and to the tests used to evaluate progress.

Math and language programs often have useful drills because the content of the drills and the tests that come up later are almost exactly the same. But to select programs in other areas where content can vary, you'll need advice from school about *what* spelling, history, government, or social studies the program should cover.

The behavioral psychologist B. F. Skinner said computer programs (he called them teaching machines in the 1960's) would take over most of the activity in the future schoolrooms of the 1980's and beyond. His prediction was right in that the programs have become a part of many classrooms and libraries, but their application is far short of Skinner's expectations. What happened?

Skinner felt that success with questions and answers would be enough incentive to keep the student working. But for most children, the novelty of working the screen wears off, and adult encouragements and real-life applications are needed to keep interest up. It's the same support from parents and teachers that homework and lessons have always required.

Leaving a student on a chair, even one in front of a computer, may not produce learning that will show up on school tests unless parents provide the encouragement that will keep the practice going.

A second limitation of computer effectiveness is in the *action* **the student is asked for.** Remember, learning is in the *doing*. If a student learns to press the right buttons on a keyboard to answer math questions, his performance will be best there and less perfect on paper and pencil tests and in verbal drills. **It's amazing to us adults that learning three plus five on a computer doesn't result in a correct answer to that question on every test paper after that.**

The student can make improvements with a computer program but **how the improvement shows up on tests depends on how similar the test is to the program, not only in content, but in the *way* the student is asked to provide answers.**

Here's another place you can contribute: make up some tests. Arrange to collect information from your child's school about what the tests are like. Then, you can construct some practice tests on the computer material, but in the format and style your student will encounter at school. Perhaps your student could make up these practice tests. Quizzes and drills with pencil and paper will give your child practice in expressing the answers as required later when no keyboard is around.

School Behaviors

Sometimes people argue that the performance by good students proves that problem students can shape up also. But we know habits change only for important reasons such as new encouragements for reasonable goals. Threats, reprimands, and coercions are temporary ways to shape up students. But if we could get the poor student consistently going right, he/she would have a good chance of encountering good results and then continuing. We need a way to get that first turn-around to work:

Ian:	*"I like war books."*
Media Specialist:	*"I know you do, but what about those homework papers you need to do?"*

| Ian: | *"Oh, I'll never catch up, so why keep trying?"* |
| Media Specialist: | *"Well, I'll give you a reason, Ian. For every finished homework paper you show me, I'll find one of those books you're interested in, or I'll have a piece of candy for you. Choose an easy paper first so that you will have some success right away."* |

This strategy helped Ian catch up in one of his classes, but should candy be used as a reward in school? Shouldn't Ian get the practice of looking up his own books in the media center? Although these are important points, I think in this case the need requires concrete rewards to get important behavior going again. Using an easy paper as a starting point was also a good suggestion.

An Additional Schoolroom Strategy

The next few suggestions are taken from my book *Teenagers and Parents,* but as you will see they can help younger children just as much. Counselors coach students to improve their classroom habits with these steps. Use incentives to encourage your child to try them also, particularly in classes where your student is "having trouble with the teacher."

1. **A student influences a teacher's attitude just as a teacher influences a student.** When there is a choice, your student should sit in a seat as close to the front as possible and keep good eye contact with the teacher during presentations, just as you would practice good listening skills in a private situation.

2. Your student should be alert for a question to ask concerning the material. A continual banter of unnecessary questions will do no good, but good questions help learning *and* teaching. **When Einstein would come home from school, his mother would say:** *"Did you ask any good questions today?"* If your student tries to ask good questions in class, she has reasons to follow the teachers' presentations more closely and is more likely to learn.

3. Your student should occasionally talk to the teacher about the subject. On at least a weekly basis, she should speak to the teacher about the class with a question or comparison to some aspect of her other subjects or experiences.

Some people may object to the contrived nature of these suggestions, but **many children have the mistaken notion that the classroom is, or should be, a place where completely passive learning takes place.** The student needs to know that an active, assertive role is necessary. The fact is that a classroom is a social situation as well as one for learning. Warming your relationship with your teacher will improve your active learning, and *that* will improve grades!

An Additional Strategy to Try at Home

A Harvard professor I know always distributes a slip of paper to each student before class. The top line on the slip reads, *"The main point of the day was . . ."* followed by a space for the student to complete the statement. The next line says, *"My question for today is . . ."* followed by more writing room. The professor collects the slips after class to see how the main point has been understood and what confusion is in need of more attention during the next class. Students must think, summarize, and question, and the professor has an excellent feedback. Many professors now use this procedure. *Even before your child goes to Harvard,* the question-and-answer game can help school work.

Try this exercise in question-asking practice: Explain that you are going to play a question and information game related to the media and school.

1. The parent picks a science news show or written article heard or seen lately and makes up a question about the information. For example, *"This morning I read an article about the eclipse tonight. What I want to know is, why does an eclipse happen sometimes and not at other times?"*

2. Now, it's the child's turn to ask a question about school subject material. Choose classes in which learning needs to be improved. For example, if geography is a problem: *"Can you point to a place on the map where four states come together?"*

   It is not necessary for either player to answer each question, but if this happens, it's a plus to the main goal of the game, which is to focus on the usefulness of each subject or media item. Repeat the game occasionally with different school subjects.

3. A follow-up to the game is for the child to ask questions in classes at school. Compliment your child for questions and encourage discussion about the information. If your child didn't ask a question, have him/her write the ones that would have been best to ask.

An Additional Strategy for Homework Time

Here's an activity that can help children find their most effective study method.

1. Both parent and child each read silently two different pages from two school texts, trying to remember as much as possible. Then they take a break to listen to 15 minutes of favorite music together while having a snack. After the break, each takes a turn telling everything remembered from the assigned page. The listener needs to take brief notes.

2. Then both parent and child read another page of school material *out loud,* trying to remember everything they can. Then they take a break to do a chore together for about 15 minutes. Then they tell each other and take notes about what each recalls.

3. In a third reading, each of you could read a page and take notes on what you read. Break for a game of cards. Share what each of you remember (without your notes). Each listener takes notes on the other's report.

4. Compare the amount of notes from each session. Which study method produced the most recall? Discuss the reasons for your results.

The more activity (reading aloud and taking notes) your student does with the study material, the more real learning he will accomplish. Evaluate these study methods and encourage your child to use the ones that work the best for him or her.

The most important advice on learning comes from early history when Sophocles said, *"The learning is in the doing of the thing."* If you wanted to improve your tennis, you would probably arrange some time to practice on the courts. If you wanted to learn some new guitar strums, you would practice them. When it comes to schoolwork, it's easy for the student to forget how much *practice counts*.

Guideline 1
Always Use Homework Time in an Active Way

Action Example 1: Always have pencil and paper handy when reading. Note-taking is good practice, and good practice is good learning. Take notes on every page of reading. For most students, staring at pages is just an excuse to put off real learning. **Publishers of school books are always struggling to keep the size and expense of books down. Every page has something to say. What is it? Write it down.**

It's a good idea to put many of these notes in question form. The student should use the headings in the book to make up the questions and use note cards if they are convenient. Note cards also encourage review of specifics. **As test time approaches, students with the note-taking habit will already have their own review to study!**

Action Example 2: Students should make new lists, drawings and summaries of class materials. Any new "doing" will help the student remember. Working with other students can produce the same kind of practice and drill. New lists, drawings and charts are more easily remembered by those who create them. **I have never had a student fail a course when he produced study notes and other evidence of practice.**

Action Example 3: Make up the test. If your students are still concerned about a test, they should construct their own version of it trying to make it as similar to the one expected as they can. Students often report that more than half of their questions were the same as the ones on the teacher's test! With those questions answered in advance, the students easily remembered their answers and were quickly half-way to a good test grade.

Action Example 4: Keep a calendar. The calendar should include: 1) plans for homework for each day, 2) a record of successes, and 3) priorities of the assignments to study so that time is spent on the most important work of the moment.

Guideline 2
Reinforce Practice

Many competing activities have built-in immediate rewards, but the benefits of studying are slow in showing up and often a long way off. But the student does become more efficient as good study skills develop—the longer you practice a habit the more reliable and useful it becomes. Future opportunities, grades and preparation for new subjects will have long-range benefits but are weak motivators for present effort.

Here's what a teacher or parent can do to reinforce a student who has not acquired the attitudes or skills to study effectively:

1. Provide a place where active note-taking is convenient. This is just as important to the learning place as freedom from distraction.
2. Talk about subjects the students are taking and create examples of the usefulness of the material.

3. Reinforce knowledge about the subjects by asking questions—even questions that stump the parents as well as the student and make it necessary to look up the answer in the homework materials.

4. Reinforce and praise daily and weekly grades.

Guideline 3
Use a Strategy for Tests

Even after students have acquired good study habits through the guidelines of their own practice and encouragement from parents and teachers, they often complain of having trouble with tests. Here are test strategies that bring positive results in either essay or objective tests.

Objective tests: Every student intends to answer each question, but very often items go unanswered. There are two reasons for this: fear of guessing and failure to remember the question! The student should carefully read *and eliminate* options. Checking off poor choices allows the student to focus on the remaining options and improve chances that small differences will be discovered. Once an answer has been selected, the student should read the question one more time to be sure that the selection is actually an answer to this particular question. Very often wrong options are, in themselves, correct, but not the answer to the initial question.

Essay tests: Answer each question twice—once in outline form and then as an essay answer. The student should write a brief outline on another sheet or in the margin before beginning essay answers. This first answer can be in the student's own words and shorthand. For example, in response to the question, *"What was important about the Gettysburg Address?"* the student might jot down, *"Lincoln, at graveyard, during Civil War, trying to unite the country, said country must try hard to finish the war, for equality and people to run government, give quote."*

Now, looking at the first answer, the student is likely to make the second answer complete and in good form. Also, as the student is writing the final answer, new points may come to mind to add to the final answer at the right places according to the outline. The teacher is more likely to give a high score when the major points are easy to find.

Learning Is a Required Activity of Life

Students often believe that if only they could get through school, the demands of learning would be over. Adults know that new learning tasks are always coming up, both on the job and at home. Many of the specifics of school lessons will be forgotten, but the means for finding and learning them again will prepare your child for most challenges.

Students with good learning and test-taking habits will always have an easier and more enjoyable experience with each new opportunity in both their work and home life.

Exercise and Summary for T-4
TEACH with Good Listening and Good Coaching

With another parent or a friend practice the rules of conversation while you share a simple story such as a shopping trip, mild difficulty getting the kids to school, or helping them with homework. Begin with one person as the listener and one as the teller. Reserve time at the end to assess how the following good communication skills were used.

1. **Keep eye contact.** Look at your conversation partner most of the time. A child expects a good listener to look at him/her. We don't like to feel unattended because the person we're trying to talk to is staring at the newspaper or TV while we ask a question. Children feel that way too.

2. **Use good posture.** Face your son or daughter while talking and listening. Use body language that says, *"I'm alert! I'm interested!"* A parent who slumps, looks away, or even *walks* away sends messages that discourage and insult the talker.

3. **Respond often with reflective and sympathetic comments, instead of evaluations.** Avoid criticism, blaming, and threatening remarks. Reword the last thing your partner said to show you understand what he/she told you. *"Boy, I really hate that Mr. Jones for math!"* could be answered with, *"He really annoys you."* or *"You get mad in there a lot, I guess."* Evaluations need to wait for invitations because they emphasize your authority (rightness) and your child's ignorance (wrongness).

4. **Ask questions frequently to show interest.** Use questions that continue the conversation by asking for longer answers than just *"yes"* or *"no." "How did it feel?"* is more likely to continue the talk than *"What time was it?"* Emphasize *IT* questions instead of using *YOU: "How was it at school today?"* not *"How did you do at school?"* Careful questions can help in a neutral, non-opinionated way, so the speaker discovers a better understanding of what happened and why.

4. **Avoid solution statements.** Replace the temptation to give advice or criticism by reflecting your partner's statements instead. Suggestions such as *"Why don't you . . .?"* or *"Have you tried . . .?"* make the one with the problem feel inferior, resentful, and argumentative. You will get the whole story by reflecting, and your listening helps because the speaker will clarify the situation and his/her feelings by telling about it.

5. **Share your experience.** Share stories, jokes, and experiences that helped you learn about getting along in life. Be selective. Avoid stories that are too close to a sore point with your child. If your son or daughter feels your experiences are not directed as advice to his\her specific weaknesses, the tales can be enjoyed and they will improve the relationship.

T - 5
TEAM UP
and Enjoy Relationships With Your Children and People Who Help

A great parent-child relationship should be a part of every day of childhood. The child longs for the joy and safety of it and parents take satisfaction and pride in it. Consistent strategies, planned with the help of other parents, are key ingredients in cultivating this relationship.

Whether you are a single parent or one-half of a partnership, child-rearing can be enjoyable and more successful with the help of the extended family of adults who influence your child.

14

Ingredients of a Great
Parent-Child Relationship

Your relationship with your child is developing
from a mixture of your understanding of what's
going on, your messages, rules, listening, and
example. This chapter lists some guidelines to
bring all of that together.

**What guidelines could measure up to the task of preparing
a child's future?** Only ones that lead the child to courageous
learning and expression without fear of unjustified criticism; ones
that will help you maintain a relationship that gives your child the
self-confidence and self-esteem to be comfortable in childhood and
competent in adulthood.

**Basic heredity and personality will still show through
childhood experiences, but a review of the daily events can
often be more useful because a parent can meet the needs, plan
to withhold reactions, and deliberately provide a positive
example.** The suggestions of the previous chapters can help you
discover your child's motivations and satisfy those wants with

strategies that work toward growth and proper behavior.

The best outcome would be that we all get what we deserve, improve our behavior as a result, and are satisfied. In the real world, of course, some justice is done, but undeserved rewards do happen, and satisfaction occurs only to a degree. Through it all, this book assumes that parents can make things come out better for themselves and their children.

> *Start early for the sake of your child's self-esteem.*

The crucial question confronting parents is not whether rewards, punishments, encouragements, and discouragements should be used to influence a child's behavior; in day-to-day living that influence is inevitable. The question is whether parents will have time and love enough to plan some of these consequences so that the child will learn what needs to be learned and grow up properly.

Start Early

The most dangerous thing on earth is a human being with nothing to do. A child may not have the potential to cause as much havoc as an adult, but a child delayed from moving on to new challenges has a surprising ability to find trouble. That is one reason this book encourages you to start expecting, encouraging, and rewarding your child to make his/her bed, cook a meal, wash the car, look after his/her younger sibling, as soon as it is reasonable. Start early for the sake of your child's self-esteem and for the sake of building abilities he/she can be proud of.

Parents are often hesitant in handing over the daily tasks of life for many reasons. They may feel a responsibility to do the chores themselves, and if they insist that the child take part, they feel guilty. Parents are often inclined to protect their children from drudgery as if it were an evil to be kept from the child as long as possible.

Include Worthwhile Chores

Completing the drudgeries of life is, in fact, one source of satisfaction that wards off depression. With children this benefit is often missed because the verbiage that goes with chores is usually negative. Both parent and child talk of "chores" as burdens to be carried. That's true, but the usefulness to psychological health should not be forgotten by the parent facing resistance from a growing-up child.

Boys, in particular, are subject to protection from chores and often suffer feelings of exasperation at having nothing "really worthwhile" to do. **Remember a child probably wouldn't know what's "really worthwhile" if it bumped him in the leg!**

Parents need to teach these values like all others, by example and by making sure that the son, as well as the daughter, gets opportunity and encouragement for his/her domestic efforts. **For a boy, unrecognized sexism may be at work in denying him training for everyday chores.** He may not know he is being short-changed. He may complain all the way through any chore requested of him. But his self-respect and his value of himself will improve with every competence he acquires. And **when he encounters a temptation to try some self-degrading, or self-damaging behavior—drugs, for example—he will be a little more likely to value himself and believe he has more to lose.**

> *When temptations come along, your child will believe he has more to lose.*

When an adult refuses, let's say, a drink at lunch, what is the most common excuse? *"Sorry, I can't, I've got to work this afternoon, things to do."* The self-evaluation is: *"I have important things to accomplish (skills to use); I am too valuable!"*

Build from Small Requests to Big Challenges

Perhaps your strategy cannot always guarantee good behavior. But you can plan situations that put the odds in your favor and ensure that there will be more opportunities for good behavior and learning.

For example, mothers know that their children get cranky or tired at certain times. So for strategies that deal with aggressive behaviors, a child has a better chance at some times than others. **While it's true the child will eventually have to learn to control himself in all situations, let's start the training at a time of day when success and opportunity for support are likely.** A child who is cranky before dinner and is just learning to control his temper with others, shouldn't have friends over in the late afternoon when probabilities for mistakes are high. Another plan might be to have dinner earlier, or lunch later, in order to give him a better chance for success.

These alternatives are not strategies about reactions and consequences but merely rearrangements of the family schedule or environment to maximize success and minimize errors. For example, accidents at mealtime can easily be influenced by the way the situation is first set up.

If a child is given a glass of milk too full, a glass of juice too hard to handle, three utensils when he only uses one, five foods to play with when he never eats three, and is then seated on two slippery telephone books, the family is set up for an unhappy dinner of trouble right from the start. The goal may be to get him to eat properly with these disadvantages, but the training will have to start with a better chance for success.

If all of this seems to be too much trouble, it may be time to rethink just how serious the problem is. These reactions may seem too extreme because it's "just not *that* important" when the parents give the problem serious thought. Maybe changing eating habits, for example, is not worth giving up all dinnertime pleasantness and everybody should eat what they want of what is served. Children, adults and creatures of the earth will pick a fairly good diet on their own if it is available and sugar is subtracted from the temptations.

Have Your Support "At the Ready"

When can you expect a child to learn without these extra incentives? And until then, how do you find the right consequence?

The answer here may lie in the question: *"What would be the result if he or she did the task right?"* This should be a frequent parental question: Has the problem come up because of a bad behavior or the absence of a good one? What are we looking for? What will we do when he or she gets it right? A parent with answers to these questions will know how to react and what to do when even a slight improvement pops out.

> *Start the training at a time of day when success and opportunity for support are likely.*

Without this soul-searching for a ready incentive when the child is *slightly* successful, the little success may not be recognized and only instant and complete triumph by the child (not likely) will produce a positive reaction.

Without help with small encouragements along the way, triumph may be so long in coming that parents will be unenthusiastic in support, *"Well, it's about time you got that room cleaned up!"* So we need an early incentive not only to encourage the child but to encourage ourselves to continue genuine and enthusiastic support. As an example of putting together a little engineering and a little support for small successes, let's look at the old "coming when called" problem. Mom cooks a good dinner, calls everyone when it's ready, and gets a *"Just a second, Mom,"* from those glued to the TV.

Three questions can help you think about how to make this situation better: 1) How can the *situation* be improved, that is, set up so that the proper and considerate behavior is more likely? 2) What will you do when they do it? 3) What should be the reaction when they don't?

We need answers to the question: What if he/she does it right?

The set-up might include delaying dinner so everyone is hungry, timing the call for dinner with the break between TV shows, and having favorites when the schedule is tight, and you want people to come on time. Your reaction when they get it right might be a simple compliment, *"Oh good, Tom, you came right away. It makes me feel good because I worked hard to have a good meal ready."*

The plan might include a few dinner conversation topics very relevant to the children. Your reaction to procrastination might include starting without the children, or prohibiting TV from 6 pm to 8 pm so you won't have the competition. **With these reactions in place, you have a plan to produce improvements—maybe not complete harmony in the household, but at least a good chance for some pleasant evenings.** Now you should have your listening skills "at the ready."

Keep Your Support Consistent
With Growing Expectations

Most parents do support their children but the planning encouraged in this book can pin down, specifically, what you want to encourage. If the encouragement is inconsistent and more related to the parent's mood than the child's actions, the child may find that playing it safe is better than trying to predict parental moods.

The lack of some thoughtful planning by parents leads to erratic reactions and makes cynics out of children. When moody and inconsistent parents do praise or reward their kids and the kids don't react with the proper appreciation, the parents are disappointed. The child may be cynical because he knows the praise is a temporary product of his parents' moods and not a consistent appreciation of his success.

If a plan for positive reactions accumulates success over a few weeks, then the next encouragements for the next success become easier to give. A respect and positive expectation for what the child will do develops, and we are off to a better relationship.

The level of expectation should be determined by what the parents know the child *will* (not could) do. But the frustration of no progress often leads parents to greater demands instead of smaller ones. This makes failure and parental disappointment even more likely next time.

> *Someone will have to be adult enough to set standards the child can, and is likely, to meet.*

What does all this make of dinner time? Either something a child will look forward to if the encouragement and listening rules are followed or something a child would just as soon be late for if criticism is likely.

Do you look forward to a dinner with Uncle George? Yes, if

he's agreeable, supportive, and engaging. No, if he's critical, punitive, and disapproving. **With Uncle George, you make your invitations accordingly.**

With your child, you'll have to *build* the situation rather than take it or leave it. Someone will have to be adult enough to set standards the child can, and is likely, to meet. Encourage the successes and build a pleasant situation.

With Uncle George, you can expect him to take some responsibility for the dinner time atmosphere. With young ones, someone else must create it. **Later, with the skills they learn from you, they can take some social responsibility themselves.**

Change the Situation Slowly

Of course, parents know that starting at the ideal is not possible, but many believe they should withhold strong encouragement until good progress is made. But a gradual approach, with encouragement for any effort, is more effective.

To guarantee support for the very first efforts a person makes on a new task, we need a short-term target. Later we can add the higher expectations by expanding the request or the range of circumstances.

Here's an example of the gradual approach: When I first met Carol she would not talk in school. Her mother had come to see me because this only-a-little-troublesome habit had become a real problem with the requirement that in order to be promoted from first grade, she had to demonstrate reading aloud in class. Fortunately for Carol, her mom, and for me, reading aloud was not part of the problem. Reading aloud was already easy for Carol to do under another circumstance, at home with her mother. Carol needed to bring her success to the school situation.

At the beginning we decided to make Carol's schoolroom

experience similar to her reading situation at home. First Mom met Carol after school. With the classroom empty, Carol would sit in her seat and read to her mother for a few minutes. The following week the teacher stayed in the classroom but was obviously occupied with her desk work in front of the room. She took no notice of Carol or the reading.

In the third week, the teacher took more notice of the mother-daughter reading session, and by the fourth week she did nothing but listen to Carol read. **For a few more sessions Mom sat farther away and the teacher sat nearer. The last session took place before the other children had left the room, and Carol's promotion to second grade was assured.**

Plan Your Shaping Steps

The procedure just described did not require new behaviors or complicated strategies. If the child had yet to learn to read, we would have had a much bigger problem, requiring many more steps along the way. We might start with identifying pictures or letters, providing some phonics training, adding simple words to the lessons, and so on.

> *Even after some progress, backtracking may be necessary to keep the positive reactions high during slumps in performance.*

Whenever you use a shaping process like this, you must begin with a level of performance that occurs frequently so that the child can learn the rules and experience some success right away. **Even after some progress, backtracking may be necessary to keep the positive reactions high during the slumps in performance.**

In nearly every case the ideal behavior is not gained in one easy step. At first you will have to dig back to some low level of success. After that not-very-exciting level has been strengthened, the next level can be added with plenty of encouragement.

Gradual Changes for Amy and Jeff

Amy came home with failure after failure on her spelling lists. Her mom's temptation was to drill her over the errors she had made and, although getting rid of error was the ultimate goal, this wouldn't do much to pump up Amy. The approach of *"Let's all help Amy with her mistakes"* ensures that rewards will be hard to come by, and the results will be frustrating and embarrassing with frequent mistakes. It will emphasize how much Mom knows and how little Amy knows.

So I asked Amy's mom to start spelling sessions with the few words Amy had right from the lists of the past weeks. Mom ran through those lists, noting with pride and encouragement all Amy's successes, which were many. Then Amy's mom mixed in a few of the ones that Amy had missed. Bolstered by some recent successes, Amy could tolerate her own errors and her mom's corrections. Mom would often come right back to one or two easier words. **Mom manipulated Amy's success rate and kept it high by putting in as many "easy" words as necessary.** A few 15-minute drills, and Amy was finished with the week's spelling and was feeling good about herself and about Mom.

> *Mom manipulated Amy's spelling success rate and kept it high by putting in as many "easy" words as necessary.*

Jeffrey is another example of starting where encouragement is probable. Jeff's mother said teachers complained that he couldn't sit still in school, keep his attention on his work, or stay out of trouble with other students. **The prospect of long-term consequences (grades, threats of failing, being held back) had no effect on him.**

By using the technique of focusing (Chapter 3) and defining the desired good behavior, we could start with some aspect of Jeff's problem, building up the time he sits in his seat with some incentive for doing so, then working on his attention span, and then his tendency to fight with other students. All this would be a long process.

But these behaviors are interrelated with the thread of Jeff's boredom so we may have to deal with them all at once. **The strategy with Jeff's teacher and parents was to concentrate on all three complaints at the same time, but only for a short period.**

Each morning Jeff's teacher "checked in" with him as he arrived in class so that he had a little attention "in the bank" to start with. Then if Jeff stayed in his seat, paid attention, and didn't get into any trouble with others for the first 15 minutes of class, he would get a reward for his success—a copy of a note printed up for his teacher to use. It said, *"Dear Mr. & Mrs. Jones, Jeffrey started school just fine today."* More about the notes later.

The strategy for Jeff required him to take control of himself all at once—quite a challenge and one that seems to violate our notion of very small steps to guarantee reward at the very beginning. But in Jeff's case we are quite demanding right from the start, but only for a *very short time*, which makes it possible to deliver on the reward very quickly. **Nothing Jeff does during the rest of the day can take away the precious note which is about how he** *started off* **his day.**

Now because it was difficult for Jeffrey's parents to deliver encouragement and support in the classroom where the success might happen, we used a part of the idea of a "token economy."

You are familiar with this idea in your own life. You work for tokens, something that is only a symbol of the value it can be exchanged for; in the real world, money.

Jeff knows about money, too, but Jeff has an extra token—the note from the teacher. Jeff was told, *"If you stay in your seat, pay attention, and stay out of trouble for the first 15 minutes of class, Mrs. Norton will give you a note, and you can use that note for extra play-time, TV time, or extra dessert at home after school."*

> *The usual results of good school behavior are going to have to take over and keep Jeff on the right track once we get him started.*

Jeff found more than one use for his notes and wanted more. A second note from the teacher was supplied for the second 15 minutes, the interval was changed to 20 minutes and two more intervals were added for the first 40 minutes after lunch. **Now Jeff could get a maximum of four notes—tickets of admission to extra activities at home—each day.**

We didn't want to complicate the teacher's procedures so Jeff's parents made up the notes and delivered them to her. And we didn't want to give extra attention to Jeff for being bad. Therefore, the teacher refrained from discussing Jeff's mistakes in class. He either got the note or he didn't—no arguments, no repeated explanations, and no threats.

We all know that a system like this can't be kept going for a long time. Jeff will get tired of it, his parents may get tired of thinking up new privileges, and the teacher certainly has enough to do without continuing this rule for a long time. The usual results of good school behavior are going to have to take over and keep Jeff on the right track once we get him started.

The natural results of admiration, encouragement, and

usefulness of his learning at home need to be emphasized, as described in Chapter 13, to gradually take the place of the contrived reward.

There are three important points of caution here. First, the teacher must be consistent and keep in mind a good definition of what 15 minutes of good behavior is. Second, Mom and Dad have to play the game strictly with Jeff. And third, Jeff must understand from the beginning that the rules will change along the way.

Jeff's case required a lot of effort from several people. They carried through, and Jeff became a much better student as a result. The planning, conferences, notes and the work at home took time and effort.

Move Along, the Children are Growing

Once some new level has been reached, the problem is how fast to move along. **Feedback and support can grow stale rapidly if you don't move on to some new and challenging target.** Also, dwelling too long at one stage can make it difficult to move on later. Consider the parent who praises baby talk long after it has been mastered. It was a necessary first level in shaping behavior, and of course support for the effort at first was just good parenting. But the longer the child continues baby talk, the more likely he is to discover that some people will always find it cute and attractive. Also his parents become very practiced at understanding it and inadvertently reward the almost unintelligible requests. These complications have their counterparts in eating, dressing, and "baby" social skills—selfishness, possessiveness, and lack of consideration for others.

Instead of a policy that says, *"You can never move too slowly,"* it is usually better to take a more flexible view of child-rearing and say, ***"When in doubt, move up to a new level of expectation for*** *awhile; you can always move back again, if necessary."*

One of the most common reasons for hesitating to move up is that the next step involves some real consequences for the parent.

> *When in doubt, move up to a new level of expectation for awhile; you can always move back again, if necessary.*

After a child has learned to count money and make change, he is ready to shop— probably with your money! This is a very dangerous time for hesitation on your part because this is when the child learns whether or not the skills are really useful and part of growing up or just boring preparation for growing up later.

In the later steps of shaping behavior, a parent's role changes. The parent has prepared the child to some extent for the outside world and now that world provides more and more of the consequences. But you still have an important duty. Now your job begins to resemble a coach's job. You're not in the game any more providing consequences; you are more often on the sidelines giving advice, pointing out what happened, and why and where the consequences are coming from.

The crucial point to remember is that this change of duty doesn't happen at a particular age, but for particular skills. You may finish giving planned lessons for toilet training by four, hopefully you'll be finished with eating behavior by eight. Really?! And you still may be working on money management at 17 and social skills at 25!

15

Team Up with Spouses, Companions, and Others Who Help

Parents with and without partners encounter new problems as child-rearing becomes *adult*-rearing. Expanding moments of separation become more apparent and the paradox of *keeping* control while also *giving it away* creates tough moments for all parents. Single parents have many disadvantages in rearing children solo. Yet they do have the advantage of a more consistent set of rules and reactions. All parents need a lot of cooperation from other family members, friends, and the community as an extended family. It *does* take a village.

Parent Abuse or Respect?
Your Friends Can Make the Difference

Friends should protect friends. That's obvious enough, but what happens in *your* home when your child mistreats *you*? Let's look at this conversation with Mom, her son Kevin, and Aunt Eileen:

Kevin:	*"I'm going to watch TV now."*
Mom:	*"What about your homework?"*
Kevin:	*"Later. I've got plenty of time."*
Mom:	*"Isn't your history paper due tomorrow?"*
Kevin:	*"Mom, you don't know anything about how long that paper will take."*
Aunt Eileen:	*"Be careful how you talk to your mother. She's had many years of school. I think she knows."*
Kevin:	*"I'll do it when I'm ready."*
Aunt Eileen:	*"Well, I can't take you to soccer practice until your Mom says you are ready."*
Kevin:	*"You didn't even know about the history paper until Mom brought it up. It's none of your business."*
Mom:	*"Don't talk to your aunt that way. She's concerned about you too. Now get to that paper so you can make your practice."*

This struggle may not end here, but Mom and Aunt Eileen, standing up for each other, are not going to take part in Kevin's divide-and-conquer strategy. They stay close, and they don't tolerate abuse from Kevin.

Your best protectors are your own relatives, friends, or spouse who come to your aid when you are mistreated—even by a child.

Two adults can be stronger than one, and they can provide a model to children about how members of the family should treat each other. ***"Say, be careful how you speak to your mother!"*** can be a source of comfort to a mom and a help to a growing child blundering into accumulating guilt:

> Jenny: *"Mom, tie my shoe!"*
> Mom: *"Just a minute, I'm talking."*
> Jenny: *"Do it now!"*
> Erica: *"Take it easy, Jenny, let your Mom finish."*
> Mom: *"Thanks, Erica. I can use that support now and then."*

How Does the Parent Abuse Habit Get Started?

A child's attitude comes from many sources, but relatives, friends, spouses and the extended family play a role from the beginning. They can make the effort to help, like Erica and Aunt Eileen, or, if they don't, they can be part of the problem. Here's Jane with her husband John:

> John: *"You can't find your keys? I can't believe it!"*
> Jane: *"Just a minute. Here they are."*
> John: *"I swear, you would lose your head if you didn't have..."*

An adult game of *"I-can't-believe-you're-such-a-klutz!"* can be easily absorbed by the kids, and **spouses or adult friends should avoid these "games."** No one can watch everything they say, but friends of parents, particularly single parents, should keep in mind the examples they set for the children. The best help a friend of a parent can give is to show a model of respect for the one doing the parenting. Here's Mom and Aunt Eileen in the car with Kevin and Jenny:

> Aunt Eileen: *"If you're going to look for a new car, you better take someone with you who knows something about it."*
>
> Mom: *"I know something about it. I have three articles right here, I've read "Buyer's Review," and I know the ratings."*
>
> Aunt Eileen: *"Oh, then you're really prepared. What do you think of these prices?"*

Aunt Eileen starts off a little negative but ends up asking Mom for information. Now, Mom needs to return the favor.

> Mom: *"How did the car you have hold up?"*

If significant others are going to help, Mom's (or Dad's) model of showing respect for the significant other needs to be part of the child's family experience. When Mom respects the opinions of others, her example improves the value of other adults in the eyes of the children.

Now, when friends or relatives show confidence in Mom's ability to do anything from driving to making financial decisions, their opinion bears added weight when the child hears it. *"What do you think about these prices?"* sends a message not only to Mom, as a parent, that her thoughts are of value, but also to any little ears in hearing range.

This is a good reason to sort out conflicts in private—away from the children. Children always have their "antennae out" and are more interested in what the conversations say about how *the people around them feel about each other* than in the content of the argument.

> John: *"This car needs some work."*
>
> Jane: *"Why don't you take it in Monday."*
>
> John: *"Me? You're the one who drives it most!"*
>
> Jane: *"I have to get to work early. You just lounge around until 8:30 anyway."*
>
> John: *"Hey, you have a cushy job..."*
>
> Jane: *"Wait, wait, let's get the car fixed, OK?"*

Both John and Jane may think this argument is about car repairs and who should see that it gets done. But a child listening on the side does not understand or even care about the details of dropping a car off for repairs. **The child is listening only to the message about the opinion each person has of the other.**

So after a simple disagreement on the car, John may be surprised to hear Jenny say: *"You don't like Mommy, do you?"*

> John: *"What? Of course I do, whatever gave you that idea?"*

The misunderstanding children get from focusing on what seems to be the feelings the adults have for each other can be corrected. But the temptation to imitate what they have heard will linger on and that can only be corrected by future examples from you—and from the Ericas, Johns, and Aunt Eileens in your child's social world.

All parents need the other adults around the family to show a positive model and message for children to hear. **Moms and Dads do not need friends or relatives around who show the children**

how to abuse their parents. That kind of friend or relative should be asked to begin changing their attitudes...or begin leaving.

Waning Parental Influence

Friends in a support group see your child less often than you do, so they can help you with new insights. Gradual changes taking place in a child going from age five to 13 are easy to miss. We often think of our children as about the same when changes are actually taking place every week and month!

The parent support group can help a mom or dad who, not recognizing growth, continue old limits on responsibilities and opportunities. **Timely changes would strengthen their son's or daughter's always-fragile self-worth.** Parents can lose influence just by neglecting the child's expanding areas of interest. So a child's complaint of "nothing to do" should be taken as more than just a complaint about the lack of amusements. It could reflect a need for useful activities that are respected in his limited adult world. **One fast way to alienate a member from a group (or family) is by not allowing him to contribute when he is ready to!**

A strange effect of sexism in our culture is that girls sometimes survive childhood better than boys because they make an earlier contribution to the family, particularly in the domestic chores. While "protecting" the male from drudgery, parents can run the risk of driving their son to find other activities that show he can "do something." **Threatened by the fact of his "worthlessness," he will cast around for a way to be proud of himself—what will he find?** Will it be a suggestion from his Mom or Dad? Or something away from his parent's influence and encouraged only by mischievous others?

Some competition for parental influence will come from a

child's expanding circle of friends who don't have to enforce any unpopular limits and who seldom reprimand or punish. Since parents do feel obligated to hold to limits that are not always popular, they begin with a disadvantage in the competition with their son's or daughter's friends.

Your parental advantage is that you know how important *positive* **support is,** and you can plan heavy doses for good behavior to a child hungry for confirmation that he/she is doing right. Parents of a child growing up need to be generous with positive support and clear about what is worthy of support.

> *Your parental advantage is that you know how important positive support is.*

But it can be tempting to continue support with no particular success in mind at all: *"I think you're wonderful even when your friends let you down!"* While support like this is often an important role for parents, it could be cruelly misleading preparation for the adult world. Parental coaching is also needed to point out the way to some solution for the child's social problems.

Talking with other parents can be helpful here. How are they reacting to new fads and habits? What good developments are they encouraging?

Actions Speak Louder

Growing up from age five to 13 brings along some new possibilities for games with parents. *"I-may-do-something-very-bad"* is a game where the child *talks* about wild intentions because of the intense reaction his parents give to it.

When you suspect this game you can try to inhibit your strong reactions to his verbal description of his intentions and concern yourself only with performance. Without a strategy, you may help create a situation where the child finds it easy to "get through" to you by making a remark about some absurd behavior he has no intention of performing.

Getting a child to "talk right" sometimes becomes the goal of the parent and the power struggle for the child. **Little talks may become unproductive because if the child starts to lose she can always agree to say (promise) what is being demanded without having to carry it through.** Threats may be made, voices raised and the child may get a good "talking to," but she will only learn to say what is expected and to avoid any genuine discussion of controversial topics.

Fat Cats

Cats seem to be one of the best animals at taking human care for granted. **Food, housing and a warm pillow, and they can ignore you for days.**

A child growing from age five to 13 may sometimes take a similar attitude. During a moment of rebellion, a child can act on the false idea that she is perfectly capable of making it on her own. Like the cat, she has been misled by a family situation that provides most of the essentials of life free and with no fanfare. You too could make it on very little if room, board, clothing, medical, and educational needs were supplied free.

The fat cat problem develops from too few demands on the child to care for herself and too few requests to contribute to the family as she acquires more ability.

As the teenage years loom not too far ahead, it's time for more realistic responsibility. But when you give more responsibility you will also need to add more incentives.

Matching Funds and Graduated Allowances

If more financial demands are to be made of a growing child, then a better means of making and using money will have to be arranged. Allowances are the major source of income for children and the teenagers they aspire to be.

A graduated allowance pays off a variable amount depending upon the behavior of the child. It uses the traditional guaranteed allowance unrelated to performance and includes responsibilities for the child to perform to earn additional amounts gradually over the week. Each time the child finishes a task, it is recorded on a chart. Each task has a value, and the accumulated amount is paid off at the end of the week.

The possible increase in allowance need not be more expensive for the family budget. As money accumulates, it doesn't all have to be spent on her amusement and stomach! Consider a matching funds program for clothes, for example, where parents may provide most of the funds, but for some items, the child contributes to the cost from his or her earnings.

Parents as Teachers, Coaches, Friends, and "Heavies"

Parental roles change with situations as well as with the ages of their children. Parents need to be aware of these changes and avoid feeling "inconsistent" when different roles are called for. Often a child's confusion over a parent's changing attitudes can be erased by a frank explanation of their mixture of perspectives.

Jack: *"Why can't we have the other cable channels. Everyone else has them."*

Mom: *"They cost more money. And not everyone has*

Jack: *them. Parents in my group say they're too expensive, too."*

Jack: *"But we're missing all the good stuff!"*

Mom: *"You see plenty of TV with its violence and ...stuff. I want you to use some of your time for useful things, where you learn something."*

Jack: *"If you were my friend, you would get the other channels."* (Sounds like a game of "If-you-loved-me,-you-would-serve-me.")

Mom: *"Jack, I <u>am</u> your friend, but sometimes I have to be a parent who is a friend and also looks out for your future. It's not easy doing both."*

Jack: *"Well, I'd be a lot happier friend if I had the other channels."*

Mom: *"Maybe so. But I have to be a parent who watches our money and watches out for your learning, as well as be a friend too. It's hard."*

Does Jack understand all this about conflicting roles? I doubt it. But he does understand that Mom cares and understands what he wants, even when she will not provide it.

Jack: *"All the kids get so noisy at soccer practice. You're the coach, you should tell them to shut up!"* (Sounds like a game of "You're-the-parent,-let-me-tell-you-your-job.")

Dad: *"Sometimes I don't want to be the heavy. If there's nothing going on at the moment, they can let go a little."*

Jack: *"I try to tell them."*

Dad: *"Hard to control the whole group. Sometimes you should try going off with a friend and just*

	doing a little passing practice until the next drill. "
Jack:	*"You're more strict with me than you are with them!"*
Dad:	*"It's different when they're not my children. Sometimes I worry more over how you are doing. For them I'm only the coach; for you I'm a parent. "*

The Rest of Your Son's or Daughter's Childhood and Your Parenthood Begins Now

In these chapters I have advocated a practical approach to child-rearing. My philosophy is that children and adults are more similar than we sometimes think. The most important similarities are that all of us deserve respect and room to learn and experiment.

> *Thoughtful and fair strategies will make your role more comfortable.*

The successful efforts of both adults and children need recognition and support to keep the progress of learning moving forward.

Both adults and children deserve the same consideration when they make mistakes. Justification for punishment is not strengthened by pointing out the young age or small stature of the victim. However, corrections, feedback, and a chance to make amends are in order for both adults and children.

Good listening habits are crucial to successful parenting. As the children grow, the more complicated the communication becomes and the importance of listening skills grows accordingly.

Along with your successful parenting should come an enjoyment of the nurturing job. Thoughtful and fair strategies will make your role more comfortable. The critical addition is consideration of your own time and needs for support and respect.

Parents need to gather adults around them who will help with the parenting job by respecting and confirming parents' rights. Sometimes Grandma or Grandpa may need to be told, *"Mom (Dad), I need your respect and help with the children. It's harder for me if your remarks suggest to the children that I am not capable."*

If your spouse or a relative lives with you, it's all the more important that you show each other the respect you expect from the children and that you come to each other's defense and aid.

Parental Teams

Most encounters in parenting are first-time experiences. Even parents with many children are usually surprised at what the next child does. **Parents need companion parents to create a situation that is both their sounding board and their think tank.** And we need the assurance that others have problems similar to ours.

Whether you are on your own, or in partnership, a parent support group can be a great help. Start a small parents' group today. Even a reluctant spouse will develop some new ideas and attitudes from a discussion group. A few calls will produce other parents who are willing to be a part. Agreement on parental strategies is *not* a requirement. The opportunity to sort through common problems is the important part, and you will probably discover everyone is partly right.

As your child becomes a teenager, the support of other parents can strengthen your stand against violence in movies, parties with alcohol, and other perils and temptations of the teen years.

For opening topics at meetings you could start with one chapter or exercise from this book. Topics suggested by other parents could be a part of each meeting.

Parenting is a hard job, but you are a natural for it. You're the one most interested in the welfare of your children, and you're close at hand every day. To enjoy successful parenting, stick to good habits, show a good model, listen, and cultivate some close advisors to discuss problems and solutions. We humans are busy with our complex lives, but we have an extra advantage: we learn well from each other. So as a final project, consider forming a group as suggested in this last exercise.

Exercise and Summary for T-5
TEAM UP with Spouses, Companions, and Other Parents

Ground Rules for Discussions
in Parent Support Groups

Parent Support Groups can provide comfort and a good sense of direction with the proper ground rules. They might also serve as a sort of extended family for your child, adding a wider circle of positive adult influences and role models in your child's life.

The following concerns are suggested as the basis for an agreement on ground rules. The first get-together of the group should discuss ground rules and come to an understanding, if not an agreement, on how each issue will be handled.

Concerning trust:
1. Emphasize confidentiality for companion parents.
2. Develop rules for telling stories on the children at group sessions and repeating them outside the session.

Concerning Consideration for Others:
3. Discuss ways to control air time
   What is fair share?
   How will we police the air time?
   How much air time for hot topics.
4. Consider the balance of topic time and social time.

Concerning the topic:
5. Discuss the selection of topics
6. Agree that the group is not an individual therapy session.
7. Agree that the group is not a couples therapy session.

Concerning General Rules:

8. Do not allow degrading of the children, even your own.
9. Emphasize that members act on their own responsibility. For example, in dealing with the schools, they do not take action in the group's name.
10. Sometimes when the ground rules are ignored, radical changes may be necessary for your child's sake.

Suggestions for Discussion for a Single Parent in the Parent Support Group

1. How can I maintain my role as *adult* and *parent*? How do others avoid using their child as a weapon against their former spouses or as a sounding board for emotional problems. How do they manage to remain strong, reliable, cheerful and loving for them.

2. Is it true that no matter how conscientiously you help a child understand the divorce or separation, at times, he/she will think it's his/her fault? How have others talked this over with their child?

3. I want to keep my life as stable and predictable as possible for my child. How are others handling current love relationships?

4. How can do others handle their relationships with their former spouse and his/her relatives? How do they let their child know that *both* his/her parents love and care about him/her.

5. How do others handle family meals together?

7. Can other parents recommend books that have effective techniques for managing the key issues of parenting?

8. How have others involved themselves and their children in civic, church or community activities? Could our group also provide an extended family network for all of us?

INDEX

Index

Handwriting, improvement of 43
Heavies, parents as 251
Heredity still shows through 229
Homework
    and allowance 112
    and parents in q and a session
      219
    and procrastinating 70
    getting h. behavior going 212
    Kim's procrastination with 74
    making up tests 221
    using h. time in active way 220
Horton 97
Hyperactive, practical approach to 6

I

Ignoring 131
    as alternative to punishment 131
    is a reaction 7
Illness, behavior during 194
Imitation
    children learn by 69
    of bad behavior 58
    of good social skills 167, 168
    of people at home and school 55
Inconvenience
    as alternative to punishment 135
    cost of 135
    principle of and Dianne's violin
      practice 137
    used to increase behavior 137
Independence, gradually expanding
    72

J

Job to do when the mood hits 78
Justification for rules 88

L

Labels
    from theories 69
    help in understanding 6
Learning by doing 40

Life philosophy learned from parents
    69
Liking
    as a behavior 52
    in social skills 167, 168
Linus syndrome 195
Lip-biting 199
Listening
    during the game(s) 180
    parents get information from 10
Listening skills 149-166
Long-term benefits, parents try to
    emphasize 48
Long-term goals, setting out 71

M

Magic bullets, there are no m. b. 80
Matching funds 251
Maximums and minumums of
    allowance 112
Mealtime reactions to behavior 10
Mealtimes, often source of parents
    complaint 186
Messages about loving and liking 52
Models to live by 55
Moodiness, reactions to 70
Musical instrumen, practice of 43

N

Nail-biting 199
Negative reinforcement 109
    as compared to punishment 109
    between spouses 110
    definition of 109
Non-Behaviors
    making plans for 49
    difficult use of 37
    rules fail time test 49

O

One-shot consequences, problems
    with 94